W9-AEL-870

Cherries in Winter

Cherries in Winter

MY FAMILY'S RECIPE
FOR HOPE IN HARD TIMES

SUZAN COLÓN

DOUBLEDAY

NEW YORK LONDON TORONTO

SYDNEY AUCKLAND

DD

DOUBLEDAY

In the great Irish tradition of storytelling, the dates aren't exact,
and the names have been changed to protect both the innocent and
the guilty, but the events are true.

All rights reserved. Published in the United States by Doubleday,
a division of Random House, Inc., New York, and in Canada
by Random House of Canada Limited, Toronto.
www.doubleday.com

DOUBLEDAY and the DD colophon are registered
trademarks of Random House, Inc.

Grateful acknowledgment is made to the following for permission to
reprint previously published material:

The Estate of Jan Struther: "Advice to My Future Grand-daughter" from
Betsinda Dances and Other Poems by Jan Struther (London: Oxford
University Press, 1931). Reprinted by permission of Ysenda
Maxtone-Graham and Robert Maxtone-Graham, on behalf of the
Estate of Jan Struther.

New York Daily News: "$5 Daily for Favorite Recipe—Chicken Roman"
from *New York Daily News*, copyright © by New York Daily News, L.P.
Reprinted by permission of *New York Daily News*.

LIBRARY OF CONGRESS CATALOGING-IN-PUBLICATION DATA
Colón, Suzan.
Cherries in winter: my family's recipe for hope in hard
times/Suzan Colón.— 1st ed.
p.cm.
1. Colón, Suzan. 2. Colón, Suzan—Family—Anecdotes.
3. Food habits—United States—Anecdotes. 4. Food habits—
Economic aspects—United States—Anecdotes. 1. Title
CT275.C7323A3 2009
394. 1'20973—dc22
2009022378

ISBN 978-0-385-53252-5

PRINTED IN THE UNITED STATES OF AMERICA

1 3 5 7 9 10 8 6 4 2

FIRST EDITION

For Mom, Dad, and Nathan

Found among Matilda's recipe file
and personal papers:

Advice to My Future Grand-daughter

While I am young and have not yet forsworn
Valor for comfort, truth for compromise
I write these words to you, the unknown, unborn
Child of the child that in this cradle lies:
"Live, then, as now I live, love as I love
With body and heart and mind, the tangled three,
Sell peace for beauty's sake, and set above
All other things—ecstasy, ecstasy."

—JAN STRUTHER

Confession

Without my illusions
I should die
Coward, I,
  Who cannot face things
  As they really are
But always seek
  The shooting star,
  The Christmas Tree
And only see
  What I want to see.

—MATILDA KALLAHER

CONTENTS

PREFACE *1*

1

YOU'RE HOME EARLY TONIGHT *11*

2

BACKBONE *17*

3

SOUP DU JOUR DÉJÀ VU *30*

4

THE LADIES OF THE GRANGE *41*

5

THE FIRST NATIONAL COFFEE CAN AND

SAVINGS BANK *48*

6

DESPERATE HOUSEWIFE *59*

7

SOUTHERN COMFORT *73*

8

HAPPY WIFE, HAPPY LIFE 95

9

HOW LONG WILL IT KEEP? 105

10

FINE VASES, CHERRIES IN WINTER, AND OTHER

LIFESAVING DEVICES 127

11

WHAT PRICE BEAUTY? 139

12

FORECAST: BLEAK TODAY, CHANCE OF THE UNIVERSE

PROVIDING TOMORROW 149

13

A TEN-DOLLAR BET AND A FIVE-DOLLAR WINNER 159

14

WE WISH YOU A MERRY TUESDAY 166

15

WHEN IN DOUBT, BAKE 175

16

FABULOUS, NEVER BETTER 189

17

LEAVE THE DISHES 198

ACKNOWLEDGMENTS 201

FAMILY TREE

Peter and Matilde Guibe
THEIR CHILDREN: *Carrie, Katie, Willie, Freddie, Nettie,
Sophie, Artie, Richie, and Madeline*

Carrie Guibe Riordan and William Riordan
THEIR CHILDREN: *Matilda, Catherine, Jack, Claire,
and Billy*

Matilda Riordan and Charles Kallaher
THEIR CHILD: *Carolyn*

*Carolyn Kallaher and E. Colón
(divorced; Carolyn later married David Granger)*
CAROLYN'S CHILD: *Suzan*

Suzan and Nathan

Note: The tree is pared down to the immediate family
members mentioned in the story.

Cherries in Winter

PREFACE

JANUARY 2009

HUDSON COUNTY, NEW JERSEY

"You know what you have to do now," my mother tells
me. "You have to put up soup."

Put up soup; that's what my family says when times
get tough. Some people batten down the hatches,
others go to the mattresses—whatever your family's
code phrase is, it means bracing yourself and doing
whatever will sustain you through rough going until
things get better. In my family, we put up soup.

That isn't just a saying, though. It means actually
getting out a big, heavy pot, like the old black cast-iron
one my grandparents made stew in, and cooking up

1

something thick and hearty that will stick to your ribs, put meat on your bones, or any of the other expressions that as a child I thought were gross—*Food sticking to my ribs? Eeew!*—but that as an adult I understand and find comforting.

So you get out your pot, and you get beans, a ham hock, a can of tomatoes. Salt, pepper, a bay leaf. Meat if you can afford it. Clams if you're near water and can dig them out at low tide like my grandpa did, raking them out of the muck and putting them in a plastic laundry basket with an inner tube around it to keep it afloat, the whole contraption tied to his waist. If there's no meat or fish, vegetables and potatoes will do.

When the soup is done, you serve it with some bread, if you have it. And you wait for things to get better. They have before, and they will again.

My family knows all about putting up soup; we've had lots of practice. But I haven't had to do it in a while, so I need a recipe.

.   .   .

It has to be here somewhere.

I'm tossing our basement like a thief, though only a thief with very practical or eccentric tastes (or both) would be interested in what's down here. I push aside the bales of toilet tissue and paper towels that my sensible husband, Nathan, buys from one of those huge box stores that feed into our "stock the bunker" mentality; once you cross the state line from New York to New Jersey, you buy in bulk. Under the paper goods are storage trunks holding clothes for better and worse weather. Another box is full of paperbacks—the novels for teenagers that I'd written a few years ago. I got extras in case literary agents, editors, or anyone else might want to see them. Like the toilet paper, they're in large supply.

Next box: My husband's old toy truck collection. I have a passing thought about what we could get for them on eBay and lingering guilt over the idea of selling part of Nathan's childhood. Under those are files from the apartment I'd lived in for almost twenty years before I got married. ("Cable Bills '82–'83"? Note to self: Find out how long Suze Orman says I have to hold on to these.) The boxes are like an archaeological excavation site—the deeper I dig, the farther back in time I go. Now I've reached the layer of partially read French textbooks from my college and high school eras. *Où est* . . . er, what I'm looking for?

Aha! In the corner of the basement is the antique trunk, the one made of wood that looks just like a pirate's chest. It could have been the prototype for the tiny replicas in fish tanks, the ones with little air bubbles that make the lid rise to reveal a plastic skeleton. The lid of this trunk, though, is weighed down with the extra cat carrier, an old hobbyhorse from the 1800s . . . Why do we have all this stuff?

The answer to that question is simple: It's because I can't bear to part with anything that belonged to my family. And this is how I know that what I'm looking for, what I'm tearing through the basement and all its boxes full of artifacts from the past and supplies for the future to find—

Is right here.

.   .   .

Inside a cardboard box in the trunk is a fraying brown accordion folder that doesn't look like much, but to my eyes it's a precious family heirloom. I tuck the treasure under my arm protectively and run back up to our apartment. Specifically, to the kitchen.

There I open the folder and get a preview whiff of what's inside: paper. Yellowing with age, yet well protected through decades of being handed down and packed, moved, unpacked, and stored in the old trunk.

Nana's recipe file.

There are pages handwritten in script so meticulous it could be a computer font, giving instructions for Aunt Nettie's Clam Chowder and German Potato Salad. There are typewritten directions for Chicken Pie à la Mississippi in both an Old-Fashioned Method and a Modern Recipe. The one for Sausage-Corn Skillet is typed on the thin airmail correspondence paper called, appropriately enough for a recipe, onionskin.

Then there are magazine and newspaper clippings, some snipped neatly along their borders, others hastily torn out. Many of these are for chicken—Chicken Marengo, Chicken Fricassee, Chicken Roman (which, the headline announces, was the $5 DAILY FOR FAVORITE RECIPE contest winner). The other big group is baked goods, at least fifty recipes for desserts such as Sky-High Lemon Pie, Mow 'Em Down Michigan Apple Pie, and a humble prune bread.

When I put them in order, the recipes are like a time line of America's eating patterns. The undated ones, and those up to the early 1940s, show that food was simple and available. I can tell when World War II came because baking directions suddenly offer creative substitutions like lard and soya flour for butter, wheat flour, and other rationed ingredients. And in the 1950s and early '60s, there are articles on how to re-create the dishes people ate while touring Europe, a trip that was considered de rigueur at the time.

Maybe we'll be able to go to Europe again someday, I think, reading the recipe for Italian Polenta and Chicken Livers from the January 1958 issue of *Charm* magazine. But this is January 2009, when over half a million people have been laid off, banks have gone under, and huge corporations are begging the government for money. Thousands of homes sit empty because their former owners couldn't afford to pay the mortgage *and* eat. Today, a woman I know—same age as I am, dresses nicely, has a job—admitted that she didn't have enough money to buy food for her dog. In the Great Recession, the idea of a vacation seems as quaint and antique a notion as the soirée described in this fifty-year-old magazine.

I got laid off a few months ago. Nathan still has his job in mechanical systems maintenance (a fancy name for "repairman"), so we're comfortably well off by recession standards. Our rent is low, half of our friends think we live decadently because we have health insurance, and our cats are fat and happy. But there have been changes beyond giving up on the idea of taking a trip, and I notice them mostly when I'm in the kitchen. Last year I shopped at Whole Foods, aka Whole Paycheck, and got takeout any night of the week I didn't feel like "making" lasagna (meaning I placed the frozen chunk made by someone else in the microwave). This year I'm at our local cut-rate supermarket with coupons in hand to buy ingredients for soup I'll make from scratch—which was what started my search for the recipe file in the first place.

Being in this recession feels like watching a nature film about the disintegration of a major polar ice shelf. Huge chunks of everything we thought was solid keep breaking apart and disappearing into an abyss, the depth of which no one knows. Fear is palpable, and worry about how much worse it's going to get is the main topic of conversation.

And yet this feeling of uncertainty—the need to cut back and hunker down, the future reduced to daily getting by—isn't all that unfamiliar to me. It's like a neighborhood I haven't been in for a while: it looks a little different, maybe some of the storefronts have changed, and I'm older now, so more easily spooked. But I know my way around this neighborhood because I grew up here—as did my parents, my grandparents, and family members even further back than that. Occasionally, we've done pretty well for ourselves. And then, well . . . then there are times like this. And worse, much worse than this.

The difficulties we've had to deal with aren't just about money (though if financial insecurity were a business, we'd be rich). Nor are they extraordinary. Every family has stories of events that range from surviving wars against any conceivable odds to being packed into the car as a child in the middle of the night for a "trip" to avoid the sheriff knocking at the door. One only has to reach back and the stories are there, tales of courage and plain dumb luck that make us shake our heads in disbelief and respect for the ones who came before us.

If my grandparents were here, I'd ask them how they got through the Great Depression, how they dealt with World War II rationing, how they kept from being eaten away by the fear of what-next in a time when the ground under your feet might house a well-stocked bomb shelter. But Nana died when I was seven, and my grandpa, who could put up a mean "stewp"—a thick, chunky soup—when I was thirteen. I was too young to remember their wisdom, or to have understood it in the first place.

But I have the file. The recipes Nana wrote and saved offer more than directions for making the comfort food that sustained my family for four generations. They're artifacts from times both good and bad—not vague references, but proof that we've been through worse than this and have come out okay. And right now, that's something I need to know.

YOU'RE HOME EARLY TONIGHT

Suzan's Rigatoni Disoccupati

[Pasta of the Unemployed]

½ lb. pasta
1 small jar prepared spaghetti sauce

*Heat a large pot of water until boiling and add half a box
of rigatoni or whatever pasta you have. Take lid off jar of
sauce and microwave for a few minutes, stirring after each
minute to check temperature. Test pasta frequently so it
doesn't get overcooked because you're a little distracted.
Drain. Put large, comforting amounts on plates. Top just-
this-side-of-mushy pasta with nuclear-hot spaghetti
sauce. Serve with Italian bread and an explanation of
why you're home so early.*

. . .

"I got laid off today," I tell Nathan.

"Oh," he says, looking to me for a sign of how he should react—*How bad is this?*

"It's fine," I say. "I'm fine. We're going to be fine."

After all, it's not as though I didn't see this coming. I've written for magazines for twenty-four years now, and there have been two recessions during that time. When the economy starts tanking, people cut back, and if they have to make a choice between food and a magazine, I go from being employed full-time to starting another stint as a freelance writer.

So, months before I got the call from Human Resources at 4:30 on a Friday afternoon (a meeting, I guessed on my way downstairs, that was probably not about a raise and a promotion; I was right), I had begun economizing. I kept a record of my expenses and was surprised to find that I was spending upward of ten dollars a day on lunch—nearly twenty if it was a bad day and I treated myself to sushi.

I stopped eating in the fancy company cafeteria and

started brown-bagging it. My lunches were simple: tuna sandwiches, salads, last night's chicken. I asked Nathan what he spent on food in a week. The amount was so startling it led me not only to make his lunches but to bake muffins and put coffee in a thermos for him to take to work as well.

Every morning, once I got from New Jersey to New York, I skipped the subway and walked the remaining mile to the office, weaving through crowds of European tourists buying Levi's jeans and tickets to *The Lion King*. The summer went by quickly, and the walk became easier when the hordes in Times Square thinned out; as markets all over the world fell with ours, I heard fewer exotic accents.

The closer I got to the glass tower where I worked, the faster I walked, like a woman hurrying to an affair so good she knows it can't last. Oh, did I love that job, and everything that went with it. I loved saying good-morning to the dignified security guards who wore not uniforms but suits and ties, and I got a thrill from going up the long escalator that was built into an indoor waterfall. I'd give myself a once-over in the mirrored elevator before stepping out onto my floor, wanting to look good when I walked past the fashion editors at their morning meeting in the conference room. I felt important as I settled down in my office— my own office, with my name on the door and a partial view: a chunk of Central Park and a sliver of East River. In between going to meetings with my bosses and editing features, I'd write about subjects that our readers, and I, found rich and meaningful. I'd always hoped to do this kind of work, and I was proud to be a part of this prestigious team. (Both staff and content were of such high caliber that a friend nicknamed the magazine "Harvard.") My job was so busy and exciting I'd almost forget about the plastic-wrapped sandwich in my bag, and why I'd felt the need to bring one instead of getting the chef's *plat du jour* in the cafeteria.

Between the two of us, Nathan and I saved about a hundred bucks a week, and I lost around five pounds with those mile sprints. I even wrote an article about my lunch savings for the magazine. (When it was published, the tuna sandwiches and leftover chicken I'd described were accompanied by recipes for Pan Bagnat and Brown Rice Salad with Salmon.) I baked on Sundays and ate a little less at night, the better to have enough for lunch the next day. At work, one of the company chiefs held a special meeting to assure us that there were no plans for salary freezes or layoffs. I kept baking.

Every little bit I did, every dollar I saved, helped me stay calm, as did rehearsing on the walk to work what I would and would not say the day the layoff came. And when it did, I was able to take the news gracefully, accept a hug from a boss relieved that I wasn't throwing a stapler at her, and pack my personal effects quickly.

. . .

Normally, eating two bowls of pasta would put me in a carb-induced coma. Tonight, after getting a six-figure pay cut, it's calmed me down enough so that I can begin to take stock.

My family's history of rainy days gave me more than enough incentive to put part of each paycheck into a savings account. It also made me frugal—to a fault, in my mother's eyes. "You need this coat," she said when we were in a department store one afternoon.

"But Mom, it costs six hundred dollars . . ."

"And it looks like it cost a thousand! Buy it, or I'm buying it for you!"

Her rationale betrayed our humble background: "In

order to make money," she said as I reluctantly handed over my credit card, "you have to look like you already have it."

Fortunately, I wasn't wearing that coat when I negotiated a freelance contract with my now former company. The monthly stipend won't be enough to retire on, but between that and my unemployment benefits, I can put my bag lady nightmares aside for a while. Another relief is that I'm not doing this alone anymore—now I have a husband who says things like "Don't worry. I've got my job. Have another cookie and relax." Together, we have enough to pay our rent and bills and to buy groceries (less expensive ones, anyway; I may need persuasion to buy fine clothes, but not fine food).

All in all, I feel relatively safe, especially when Mom tells me about what Nana went through during her childhood and the Depression. By those standards, I'm nowhere near trouble.

2

BACKE ONE

OCTOBER 2008

WESTCHESTER, NEW YORK

Mom's Version of Great-Great-Grandmother
Matilde's Baked Pork Chops with Sauerkraut

*One loin of pork, about 1½ lbs (More than enough to serve
three)*
Seasoned salt
Olive oil and butter for sautéing
One 1-lb. bag of sauerkraut
Caraway seeds
White wine
One jar unsweetened applesauce

Preheat oven to 325 degrees. Cut loin of pork into 1½-inch-thick chops. Sprinkle chops with all-purpose seasoned salt, the kind in the large container found in the Ethnic Foods aisle of the supermarket. "Much cheaper than whatever the name-brand was I used to get," Mom says, "and God knows these days every cent counts." *Put a little olive oil in a large roasting pan and bake seasoned chops for about 45 minutes. While the chops are baking, make the sauerkraut—one bag. Melt about a tablespoon of butter in a large pan on a low flame. Sauté the sauerkraut and add a few shakes of caraway seeds.*

"How much?" I ask.

"Oh, you know . . . enough," she says. I've come to my parents' house for information about Nana and her recipes, but I should've known better than to expect exact amounts from Mom. These instructions weren't written down but handed down, all the way from my great-great-grandmother. Besides, my mother cooks by instinct, while I have to measure everything to the last grain. I'd say it was 1½ tablespoons, but it depends on how caraway-y you like your sauerkraut.

Add a slosh or two of white wine (again with the non-measurements! It looked like a quarter cup) *and about ½ cup* (or so) *of applesauce.*

By this time your pork chops should have browned
nicely, so take a good caramelized-looking one out of the
oven and add it to the pan of sautéing sauerkraut for flavor.
"Grandpa used to make this as a pork loin," Mom says
as she stirs it all around, "and he'd cut a chop off the
end to add to the sauerkraut. One day I said, 'Does it
make any sense to do that when the chop in the kraut
is the one we all fight over?' He thought about it for a
second and said, 'Good point.'" *Which is why you'll now*
add the chop with the sauerkraut and applesauce mixture
to the rest of the pork in the roasting pan. Turn the chops
over and loosen all the good browned bits on the bottom of
the pan with a wooden spoon to mix with the sauerkraut.
And back it all goes in the oven.

"For how long?" I ask.

"A while," Mom says. "You know, your Nana,
Matilda, had always wanted to write about her life.
Then *A Tree Grows in Brooklyn* came out." There were
so many similarities between Matilda and Francie, the
child heroine who grew up in working-class Brooklyn
in the early 1900s, Mom says, that Nana felt as though
her biography had already been written.

I have a vague knowledge of Nana's rough background, but it doesn't match up with the way I

remember her. She was tall, with elegantly coiffed white hair and tasteful style. She would have looked more appropriate getting out of a taxi on Fifth Avenue than off the subway at the last stop in the Bronx. And whatever poverty of affection she might have endured as a child she made up for by lavishing me with a vast, unconditional love.

"That book was someone else's story," I say. "I want to hear hers. Ours."

So, as the pork chops make comforting sizzling noises in the oven (for about another forty-five minutes), Mom and I sit in her small dining room, and she tells me the stories that Nana told her while she made dinner in their kitchen.

. . .

AUGUST 1913

THE BRONX, NEW YORK

As a child, Matilda was blissfully unaware that her father was a drunkard who wanted nothing to do with her, or why her family sometimes had nothing more than mashed potatoes and coffee for dinner. She thrived in the soil in which she was planted—she had a grandfather who doted on her, a nurturing teacher, and a bunch of neighbor kids who lived as she did, in tenements crowded with relatives. Many years later she would write about her blue-collar Bronx, New York, home:

I've always felt that it was a privilege to be poor in that neighborhood—we had such fun. The street was our playground, from double Dutch in the spring, to our dawdling steps to school as the summer approached, to the wonderful vacations when the firemen would open the hydrant and block off the street. It was our beach. We would run upstairs and put on our 80-cent striped wool bathing suits, tear down the five flights, duck under the shower, and sit on the curb drying in the sun. It was heaven. I think I went to the beach once when I was a child, to Coney Island It was fun, but I preferred the beach on my old block, right under the shadow of the Third Avenue El. I have never enjoyed anything more in all my life.

Her family, the Guibes, lived in a tenement filled with Irish and German immigrants, where the scent of corned beef and cabbage mingled in the hallways with the aroma of pork, sauerkraut, and simmering apples—a recipe Matilda's grandmother, Matilde

Guibe, brought with her to America from Alsace-Lorraine, a French region that borders on Germany.

The elder Matilde was a handsome woman who stood six feet tall, ran the family tavern, and once chased her husband, Peter, down the street and stabbed him in the backside with a meat fork during an argument. But giving birth to thirteen children weakened her heart, and having to bury five of them while they were still babies nearly broke it. When giving birth to the last one, Madeline, nearly killed Matilde, the eldest daughter, Carrie, was taken out of school in the fourth grade to stay home and care for her mother. She became nurse, cook, babysitter, and housekeeper and spent the rest of her childhood watching her siblings go to school, play with friends, meet suitors, and marry.

As the years went by, several men asked Peter Guibe for his daughter's hand, but he never consented, either because it was more convenient to keep Carrie at home, or because he respected his daughter's wish not to be married off to someone she didn't love.

Matilda would eventually write about her childhood and family, and in one of the stories, she described her mother, Carrie:

*She was a young woman who had absolutely nothing in
her life. She had a tendency to weight. She was good and
kind, but not light, not frothy, not a dancer. She had an
infinite sadness about her, and a most beautiful mouth. It
was almost perfectly shaped and had a vulnerability about
it that was heartbreaking.*

. . .

The Guibes were staunch Lutherans, and they were
shocked when Carrie, twenty-eight years old and
unwed, became pregnant. The man responsible for her
condition was William Riordan, the black sheep of a
respected family in Jersey City. For some reason, Carrie
and William weren't forced to marry at that point;
perhaps Peter disapproved of the cad so much that he
preferred his favorite daughter have her illegitimate
child quietly and be done with him. And so, on a fiercely
hot day in August of 1913, Carrie had Matilda, named for
her grandmother. Peter's instincts about Riordan had
been correct. When Carrie's brothers escorted the new
father to the hospital to see his daughter, Riordan looked
at the baby and said, "Well, I doubt that that's my kid."

The bitterness festering in Peter about how his
granddaughter had come to be—for a churchgoing

man, he had some pretty ungodly thoughts about Riordan—disappeared in the face of Matilda's existence: He adored her. She became her grandpa's pet and tiny kindred spirit. By the time she was five she'd earned him bragging rights by learning to read his copies of the *New York Times*, and she knew how to play pinochle just by watching the family on their weekly card nights. (She never did master a poker face, though, so her aunt Katie would drag her away from the game to embroider doilies for the kitchen shelves.)

Matilda and her grandpa had a routine: Every day when he was due home from work, she'd go to meet him at the train station with his beer pail in hand. For a while the family owned a tavern, but Grandpa, who worked as a stonemason, didn't drink there (which might have had something to do with whatever had led Matilde to chase him with that meat fork). Peter would go into the tavern and get his pail filled, and then he'd let Matilda carry it home so she could swing it over her head, around and around, without losing a drop.

Sometimes Matilda would walk home from school with her second-grade teacher, Miss Bumstead, who wore a grey squirrel coat that Matilda would rub against her cheek before bringing it to her from the cloakroom. Miss Bumstead lived with her father, a doctor, just around the corner from the Guibes, but in a different world. Alexander Avenue was where the "lace curtain" Irish lived—doctors, lawyers, and politicians, each family in a five-story brownstone that they owned. Housemaids scrubbed the stoops and sidewalks in front of the buildings every morning, and the brass railings and windows shone.

One afternoon, Miss Bumstead invited Matilda in. The house smelled of clean starched curtains and ginger cookies cooling on top of the coal range. Matilda's feet sank into deep carpets as she walked through suites of rooms and past shelves filled with books. Miss Bumstead's room overlooked a small garden in the back, and even the maid, who served them milk and cookies on a tray, had a beautiful little apartment.

Matilda went back to her tenement on Willis Avenue and up the five flights of cabbage-smelling stairways. Now she'd seen how other people lived. Far from being discouraged by her humble background and surroundings, she was inspired: She decided she would go to college, become a teacher like the lovely Miss Bumstead, and make something of herself.

In my family, Nana wrote, *schooling was merely something that had to be done until each child was able to go to work*. For Matilda, that was when she turned fourteen.

Grandpa had passed away that year, Grandma was long gone, and all her aunts and uncles had gotten married and moved out. Rather than live with Carrie and Riordan, who'd been forced to wed when Carrie became pregnant again, Matilda moved in with her aunt Madeline and Madeline's husband Hilding. When the legal requirements for school had been met, Matilda was sent to Bird's Business School to learn how to be a secretary. College was never a possibility.

One of her cousins had a connection at the McCrory Stores Corporation, and an application was filled out for Matilda, who was not quite sixteen, listing her age as eighteen. In July of 1929 she started her job as a secretary to one of the vice presidents at a salary of nine dollars a week.

In the building near the office Matilda worked in was another company that looked identical to hers—rows of men in offices, and women, their secretaries, making brief appearances to take dictation. She could see in the window a couple of floors up from her own, and the man at the desk would grin at her and wave. *He's flirting with me!* she thought. Matilda looked down quickly the first few times, smiling to herself. But the man was handsome, and it was nice to have a distraction from work. So after a while she'd smile and wave back.

One day in October she looked up to see him standing on the ledge outside his office. He waved to her as he always did, and then he jumped, falling several stories to the alley below.

During the Depression, Matilda was the only member of the family who was able to keep a job. Though her wages were considered good for the time, they were stretched to the limit after rent, train fare to and from the city to get to work, and food for the family. More often than not, Matilda had to get by on a corn muffin—half for breakfast and half for lunch, with coffee to keep her going—and a can of soup for dinner. She began to feel faint, her heart skipping beats before her vision went grey around the edges.

At times she looked longingly at the stove, not as much for want of food but to rest her head in the oven and turn on the gas.

. . .

"But she got through it," Mom says as she checks the pork chops, sees that they're done, and starts dishing them out of the roasting pan. "I don't know how, because the Depression almost did her in. She supported Aunt Madeline, Uncle Hil, and their baby, Evelyn, while she was just a kid and suffering from malnutrition. But she got through it. Somehow, she had the backbone to keep going and get through."

Mom puts out our plates, just two tonight since my stepdad is away on business and we're having a girls' night in. At another time I might have found this story about my grandmother depressing. It makes me ache for her; how frightened she must have been, given the amount of pressure she was under. But Nana did indeed get through a time of great despair and difficulty. Day after day, she did what she had to do, without complaint. (That's a fact: Whenever people asked her how she was, Nana would say, "Fabulous! Never better," no matter what was really going on in her life—and sometimes, there was a lot going on. Her reasoning was that complaining just kept a person miserable

and did nothing to improve the situation they were
upset about.)

What Mom said is true: Nana had backbone. My
mother and I would not be here tonight, cooking
a recipe handed down from my grandmother's
grandmother, if not for that. This isn't a sad story,
I realize—it's a strong story. I don't know if it's in me,
this backbone, but a story like this could help me to
build one.

The pork chops are salty and bronze, crackling on
the outside and filled with juicy life on the inside, and
the applesauce sweetens the tart bite of the sauerkraut.
It's sturdy food that gets you through.

3

SOUP DU JOUR DÉJÀ VU

Suzan's Attempted Split Pea Soup

One 16-oz. bag of dried split peas
3 vegetable stock cubes
1 teaspoon of oregano
1 bay leaf
1 medium-sized onion, chopped
1 carrot, chopped
1 sweet potato, chopped
Salt and pepper to taste

Put split peas in a slow cooker with six cups of water and
vegetable stock cubes. Turn cooker on low and go write an
essay you hope will be accepted at one of the magazines

*you're trying to work for. Stir occasionally to mix stock
cubes when you get stuck on a sentence.*

*Three hours later, come back to the soup and add
oregano, bay leaf, chopped onion, and chopped carrot.
Wonder why the soup looks so thin and watery and add
chopped sweet potato.*

"Sweet potato?" Mom asks when she calls to see
how I'm doing. "That's interesting." She's not saying
it sarcastically, just wondering.

*Go back to your article for an hour. Feel good about
having written most of it. Remind yourself that work has
been slow and money tight before, and you've always done
fine. Stir soup occasionally, marveling at how it really is
getting thicker—now it looks like the kind of soup that could
get you through a long, lean winter. Serve with homemade
corn bread.*

Hot Dog Soup

*Slit two hot dogs down the middle and fry in a dry pan
over medium heat until both sides are browned as you like
them. Cut into small pieces and add to the split pea soup
you made last week that you were so proud of.*

"It cost under five dollars to make three quarts of soup!" I'd told Nathan excitedly.

But after days of eating this pea porridge, even with the corn bread I baked to go with it, I wonder whether a person can go insane due to repeated ingestion of the same meal. Besides, I opened the hot dog package four days ago and I'm going to lose the remaining three, and wasting food these days is nearly as sinful as it was in Nana and Grandpa's time. Another magazine folded last week, more and more people are getting laid off from my former company, even freelancers, and I have absolutely no idea—none!—where the next job is coming from. So I hope that the hot dog pieces are close enough to ham and make the pea soup taste even a little bit different.

Heat soup for a few minutes on a low flame and serve with the last chunk of homemade corn bread. (Note: Toasting corn bread can mask staleness.) Marvel at how strangely, surprisingly comforting the hot dog pieces are in the soup, like something a little kid would get for lunch. Feel that somehow, all will be okay.

Check e-mail. Feel triumphant that you've gotten a response from your editor saying yes, she would like to see that essay, thank you very much.

NOVEMBER 2008

HUDSON COUNTY, NEW JERSEY

"I sold a story today!" I tell Nathan when he comes
home from work. In a celebratory mood, I'm making a
big dinner: roasted chicken with leeks, sweet potatoes,
and apples over wide egg noodles.

"That's great!" he says. "When will you get paid?"

"In a couple of months," I say. "It won't be much,
but it's better than nothing." The magazine, which I've
been working with for ten years, told me that due to
cutbacks, they could afford to pay me only half the
usual rate and would understand if I had to turn them
down. I accepted the fee after doing some creative
accounting: multiplied by scarcity of work and added
to the lack of steady income, it suddenly sounded like
a lot of money.

. . .

Nana was in love with words. In school she read the
dictionary, a page a day, and she bought new, updated
dictionaries the way some people buy novels. In the
box with the recipe file I find envelopes and folders

full of papers—some related to her work as a secretary for the Triborough Bridge and Tunnel Authority and the Coliseum, a convention center in New York. But most of it is her personal writing. She didn't keep a diary but wrote about her life in a series of essays and articles she hoped to send to magazines, and her Everywoman subject matter was ahead of its time. In the 1950s she wrote about returning to work after being a stay-at-home mom; finding a lump in her breast and how to prepare for the four-day hospital stay that the biopsy required back then; and dealing with a teenager who could be a handful. There's also a guide to secretarial survival entitled "You Have to Be a Bitch to Get Ahead!" That one must have been destined for *Cosmopolitan.*

She wrote a volume of poetry called *Lyrics for Losers* and a children's story, which I think is the only piece she actually submitted for publication. It received a terse reply: "We are unable to find a place for it in our publishing program." She didn't let that discourage her. She kept writing, chronicling the events of her life in would-be book chapters and entertaining herself and my mother, who was a child at the time, with her *Nutty Nursery Rhymes*:

Peas porridge hot
Peas porridge cold
Peas porridge in the pot
Nine days old—
Ugh.

I know now, from what Mom told me, how much Nana had wanted to stay in school and go on to college. But I'd never known until finding all these articles, poems, and chapters for books that would never be published how much Nana loved to write. She would probably have eaten pea soup every day for the rest of her life if she could have been a writer, even a laid-off one. I've always loved what I do, but now I approach even a small assignment with a large amount of gratitude.

    * * *

As far as food is concerned, I write about it a lot better than I can cook it. In fact, my editors at the magazine said that one of my best articles was the one about ruining Nathan's birthday dinner. I was glad something good came out of those grey, overcooked tuna steaks and that firm, underdone cauliflower.

When I lived alone, it never mattered much that I couldn't cook. I had dinners out with friends, or I ate single-girl food—steamed vegetables and brown rice from the Chinese restaurant around the corner. (I went there so frequently that one night the manager said, "Where were you yesterday? We got worried.") Now that I'm married and the one who does the cooking—especially since I'm home all the time— I want to cook well. Or, given my lack of natural talent, better.

I like to say that I never really learned how to cook because I was like Nana; we both started working from a young age and, as a result, knew our way around an office much better than a kitchen. This is a flimsy excuse, though, because Mom became a secretary at the same age that I did, and she's always been a natural cook. Give her spices she's never worked with before, and the scallops will sing.

"You have your Nana's hands," Mom has told me for as long as I can remember. Even though Nana died a long time ago, it's odd that I don't remember her hands because they were always in my small sphere—holding me, pouring out a bowl of Frosted Flakes into my own special bowl, clutching one of my miniature versions of hers while we watched *Chiller Theater* on Saturday nights.

Then my mother will hold one of her hands next to mine and say, "See, I have Grandpa's hands—big, strong, man hands." I remember his more vividly, maybe since Grandpa outlived Nana by seven years. I remember them gutting the bluefish he'd just caught for our dinner; I remember how precisely those huge hands poured his nightly shot of whiskey; I remember him clapping one of them, palms smooth from years of farm and construction work, over my burning ear after I pulled a birthday cake too close and my hair caught fire.

And Mom will sigh, "You and Nana have the same long, slim fingers, the same beautiful nails—hands that should play a piano." Neither of us ever did; instead our fingers played typewriter keys. She'd had no choice in the matter, but when I graduated from high school with purple hair, average grades, and zero plans, I simply lacked direction. "I don't know what I want to do," I mumbled.

"Then you're going to secretarial school," Mom said.

"What? Why?"

"So you can learn what you *don't* want to do."

I had the benefit of being trained on an electric typewriter. Nana had to learn on a manual machine, yet she was always the fastest and most accurate typist in any of the offices she worked in (those long piano fingers).

Which is likely why, as Mom and I read Nana's recipes—most of them typed single-spaced on her manual typewriter in the days before Wite-Out and correction tape—we notice that there is maybe one mistake on a page here or there. Among the typed pages, yellowing at the edges but otherwise in perfect condition, are a few worn-looking handwritten recipes.

"How come she typed most of these?" I ask.

Mom takes one of the pages and brings it close, lowering her glasses to get a better look. Then she smiles and nods as the memories come back. "These," she says, "are the ones from the Ladies of The Grange."

SNOWBOUND STEAK, A LA MONTANA

To make a snowbound steak, you need first a good piece
of steak. A T-Bone or Sirloin, at least one-inch thick.
First of all, you season the steak lightly on both sides
with salt and pepper. Then, using a meat hammer or some
other such device, you pound flour into the steak until it
just won't hold anymore. But, remember....the steak must
be thoroughly saturated with flour. As in the case of all
good steaks, the cooking is the most important factor of
all. So give special attention to these cooking details.
They should be followed to the letter, or your snowbound
steak won't be worth the effort. First of all, you heat
a well-greased frying pan or griddle until it's sizzling
hot. Then you place the flour saturated steak in the pan
and sear until it is golden brown....about 1 minute on each
side. Be sure the pan is good and hot so that the juices
and flavor will be sealed in during the cooking which is to
follow. After searing the steak, turn the heat down, cover
the steak and cook it until it is done. This usually requires just about 10 minutes cooking. And, remember, the
steak should be turned once during the process. When the
steak is cooked, lift it onto a platter and use the fat,
steak juices and the residue of the flour in the frying
pan to make delivious country cream gravy.

4

THE LADIES OF THE GRANGE

Snowbound Steak, à la Montana

*To make a snowbound steak, you need first a good piece of
steak. A T-bone or Sirloin, at least one-inch thick. First of
all, you season the steak lightly on both sides with salt and
pepper. Then, using a meat hammer or some other such
device, you pound flour into the steak until it just won't
hold any more. But, remember . . . the steak must be
thoroughly saturated with flour. As in the case of all good
steaks, the cooking is the most important factor of all. So
give special attention to these cooking details. They should
be followed to the letter, or your snowbound steak won't be
worth the effort. Heat a well-greased frying pan or griddle
until it's sizzling hot. Then you place the flour-saturated*

steak in the pan and sear until it is golden brown . . .
about 1 minute on each side. Be sure the pan is good and
hot so that the juices and flavor will be sealed in during
the cooking which is to follow. After searing the steak, turn
the heat down, cover the steak, and cook it until it is done.
This usually requires just about 10 minutes cooking. And,
remember, the steak should be turned once during the
process. When the steak is cooked, lift it onto a platter and
use the fat, steak juices, and the residue of the flour in the
frying pan to make delivious [sic] *country cream gravy.*

. . .

NOVEMBER 1944
SARATOGA, NEW YORK

Matilda knew how to make a few simple dishes, like
roast chicken and German potato salad, from watching
her mother. But her experience in the kitchen really
started when her husband, Charlie, came home early
from work one day and said, "Tillie, I've bought a
farm."

Charles Patrick Kallaher, an Irishman born on
Saint Patrick's Day, had at one time trained to be a
prizefighter but went into a more sensible (albeit

slightly less glamorous) line of work as a milkman. This decision served him well during the Depression, but years later, after the owner of the dairy company promoted his son to foreman, Charlie walked out. When he heard about a 200-acre spread available in Saratoga Springs in upstate New York, Charlie had a vision of himself and his family living off the land.

The first Matilda saw of the family's new home was the day in September of 1944 when she, Charlie, and two-year-old Carolyn moved into the twenty-three-room farmhouse that had been built during the Revolutionary War. They drove through an orchard of apple trees and past wildly, almost menacingly, overgrown berry bushes up to the main house. The crumbling building had fireplaces for heat, a pump for water, and an outhouse in the garden. The kitchen was in the servants' quarters and consisted of a wall-length hearth with compartments to warm, cook, or bake. (Later, they'd upgrade to a wood-burning stove.)

Charlie, ready to be a farmer, went out and bought five hundred chicks, eight dairy cows, two horses, and a herding dog.

His bucolic fantasy was short-lived. The land had gone fallow, having not been actively worked for years.

and the soil was too rocky to plant. Nor were the horses much good at plowing; one had the slow lope of a mule, and the other took off like a refugee from the Saratoga Racetrack. Faced with a barren field, the cows took it upon themselves to wander up the road to the neighbor's farm, where they feasted on the lush front lawn and shat in the newly bald patches. They were roaming free in the first place because nearly all the stone fences on the farm had fallen down, and the dog, Happy, had never actually been trained to herd animals—he preferred to wait by the side of the main road to chase cars. Matilda, meanwhile, was trying to figure out how to cook meals in a 150-year-old hearth, and September in Saratoga was starting to feel like the dead of winter had in the Bronx.

"You've got to do something," Matilda said, "or we're going to be the only farmers in Saratoga who starve to death."

"Jesus H.," Charlie swore, shaking his head. "All right. I'll go down to the factory and see what they've got." What they had was the night shift, so Charlie started commuting thirty-five miles to work each sundown.

As fall approached, deer began sauntering into the apple orchard and eating the bark off the trees. "It's Bambi!" Carolyn said excitedly. Charlie threatened to shoot them, so while he was at work, Matilda put out some of the cows' feed for the deer. "There,' she said to Carolyn, "now they won't kill the trees, your father won't kill them, and everybody's happy." The plan worked fine during the week, but the jig was up on Saturday, when Charlie was home and wondering aloud why the deer were waiting patiently by a bucket outside the barn.

One morning Matilda was washing dishes in a pail full of water that she'd dragged in from the pump when she heard the cows heading up to the neighbor's yard. She ran after them with a switch, screaming. "Get back, Evelyn! Go home, Madeline!"—many of them having been named for the relatives in the Bronx whom she missed.

But the cows were determined, and Matilda found herself apologizing again to the owner of the neighboring farm, Truman. Matilda was so pretty that Truman would just laugh it off. But in the early mornings, when he was driving his butter-and-egg route to town and caught Charlie on his way home from the night shift, he'd give him an earful. "You've got to mend those fences of yours, Charlie!"

On one of the days Matilda was trying to beat the cows back from Truman's lawn, Blanche, Truman's wife, came out and asked Matilda if she and Charlie would like to join the local branch of The Grange, the national farmers' organization. "You'll get to know some more people in the area," Blanche said. "You should come."

So they did. Truman took Charlie to meet the men, while Blanche introduced Matilda to the other farmers' wives. She didn't exactly fit right in. The women were friendly enough, but they stared, and after the first few introductions, Matilda figured out why. Still new to farm life, she was wearing her city clothes and makeup. Some of the ladies commented on her pretty hairstyle. When she shook their hands, she noticed the contrast between their bare fingers and her painted nails. She looked at the women around her, who were dressed in neat but sturdy clothing and who probably wore lipstick once a year for a wedding or a funeral. "And they were looking at me," she would later tell my mother, "like I'd just dropped in from outer space."

One of the activities of the Service and Hospitality Committee of The Grange was the sharing of recipes. One woman had a recipe for baked beans; another, for Virginia Batter Bread. "Do you have something you can contribute, Matilda?" asked the woman leading the meeting.

Matilda couldn't think of anything she knew that these women didn't, as far as cooking went. Unsure of what to say, she looked down at her red fingernails for a second and suddenly had an idea. A risky one, she thought, but what did she have to lose? *More* nothing?

"Tell you what," Matilda said. "I'll make a deal with you: You teach me how to cook, bake, and can, and I'll do your hair and makeup. What do you say?"

And this, Mom tells me, is the origin of all the neatly typed pages of recipes in the file: Apple Crunch. Quick Apple Cake. Swedish Meatballs. Rolled Shoulder of Lamb. Chicken Pie à la Mississippi, Old-Fashioned Method and Modern Recipe. Making Bread at Home— Rolls, Lesson II for Homemakers. The Grange ladies dictated their recipes, and Nana typed their words almost perfectly as she collected their instructions.

And the farm women of Saratoga Springs began to look a little prettier that winter.

5

Mom's Liver with Bacon and Onions

4–6 slices of bacon
1–2 onions, sliced
1 lb. calves' liver

*Cook bacon in a pan. Remove and drain on paper towels.
Use bacon fat to sauté onions until golden. Put cooked
onions with bacon. Use remaining fat to sauté calves' liver,
turning after a while, until cooked through. Put bacon and
onions on top of liver and serve to petulant child.*

. . .

I haven't wanted to look at my 401(k) statements for a while now, afraid of what I'll see. But all the financial experts say that I should, so I gather my courage and rip open the envelopes.

I remember how I went to the maximum allowable contribution last year, comfortably well off enough to be able to do that without even really feeling it. Now the account looks as though I hadn't made any contribution at all. Anyone who followed the rules and did what they were supposed to do has gotten screwed in the collapse of the stock market, so reading my monthly statements is yet another piece of financial advice I can go back to ignoring.

The state of my retirement plan brings to light something else I haven't wanted to face. I've been telling myself that everything is fine because I exceeded the recommended six months' worth of living expenses one is supposed to have set aside in case of emergency. I saved enough to live on for a year, as long as Nathan and I don't get any fancy ideas about going to high tea at the St. Regis. The problem is what comes after a year.

When the Great Depression started, did Nana think it would be over soon, as politicians were no doubt trying to reassure the frightened public? My 401(k) and my savings account were meant to bolster my income when I got older—I stopped saying "when I retire" a while ago, when Nathan and I realized that retirement is probably out of the question for our generation, even though we live modestly. Now it's out of the question for my parents as well; they can't see a day when they'll be able to afford to stop working.

No one knows how long this "economic situation," as the financial experts call it, will last, or what life will be like when the dust settles. This explains why I've been doing things like making Recession tea—letting a teabag steep for half the time it should so I can use it again for a second cup later, which I have with the other half of a home-baked muffin. It ain't high tea at the St. Regis, but it'll have to do for now.

.   .   .

"Are we heading for another *Depression*?" a morning news anchor intones dramatically over scenes of frantic customers banging on a failed bank's doors. Some of them brought suitcases so they could withdraw all their money. Nathan, who's watching the little TV in the kitchen while sitting at the counter, stops eating his bagel in mid-bite We've never seen anything like this in our lifetime; it looks like the part in *It's a Wonderful Life* where the townspeople mob the Bailey Building and Loan—except it's real.

I don't recognize the name of the bank that failed today—it's not one of the big ones getting bailed out by the government—and to me it doesn't look like much of a bank. These days, my idea of a safe place to keep money is a Chock full o'Nuts coffee can.

Coffee cans were a fixture in both my grandparents' home in the Bronx and in my mother's apartment in Manhattan, but for different reasons. In the fall, Grandpa started saving up bacon fat, pouring it from the skillet into an empty coffee can and storing it in the fridge to harden and keep. It got bitingly cold by the shore, and sometimes the water froze over. During the greyest days of winter, Grandpa would take the fat-filled can and a bag of bread ends and go to the water's edge. The seagulls knew him and when they saw him coming they'd swoop overhead, waiting. Grandpa used the stale bread to scoop up the bacon fat from the coffee can, and he tossed the pieces up, laughing as the seagulls caught them in midair and gulped them down. "The fat will keep them from freezing to death," he explained.

Back in the city, my mother used a coffee can for another kind of sustenance: "We're saving up for a vacation," she announced one day. "Every bit of spare money we have is going into this can."

It occurs to me now that we didn't exactly have much in the way of spare money in those days. My parents divorced when I was two, and most of our bills couldn't get paid on my single mother's salary until the words FINAL NOTICE appeared at the top. We lived in a small one-bedroom apartment where the living room doubled as Mom's bedroom and our dining room, depending on whether the convertible couch was opened or one side of the drop-leaf table was up. When I told her our television was broken, Mom said we couldn't afford to fix it. "What am I supposed to do until you get home?" I whined. "Go to the library," she said in a voice filled with warning, "and get a book." (My reading level shot up from fifth-grade to high school level that year.) Since economizing was our regular way of life, what Mom meant was that we were going to cut back even more than we usually did.

* *

"I won't eat it."

"It's good," Mom said, trying to entice me.

"I hate liver."

Now her tone was stern. "You want to go on a vacation? Eat the liver."

"What's so great about Bermuda anyway?" I pouted, picking the bacon off the offending organ meat.

"Don't know," Mom said. "That's what we're going to find out."

The couple of dollars she saved by buying liver instead of ground beef—every Tuesday and Thursday night—went right into the coffee can, as did our movie money. Before the TV broke, I had to be content with watching giant rats swarm a model of a cabin in *The Food of the Gods* on Channel 7's 4:30

Movie instead of joining my friends for the latest *Planet of the Apes* installment. For her part, Mom took the bus and the subway to work instead of treating herself to a cab in bad weather. Every dollar, quarter, dime, and my penny collection went into that coffee can.

By fall of the following year, we had enough money for our Bermuda vacation, and off we went on our big trip—not only my first plane ride, but Mom's as well. We were so excited, and every bit of scrimping and saving we'd done seemed to be worth it. We even had a little extra left over since the plane tickets and hotel had been cheaper than Mom had expected. Nobody mentioned that rates to tropical locations usually *are* lower during the hurricane season.

We were trapped in the hotel room with no television but plenty of entertainment in the form of gale-force winds knocking down palm trees outside, along with some hail. Not that we saw any of this—metal storm shutters were sealed tight behind the tropical flower-print curtains. We sat in that tiny space reading, rereading, and re-rereading the local newspaper that had been left before deliveries were halted due to the weather.

After three days we'd had enough, and the skies were clear enough for us to fly home. The only things I remember from that trip are how sweet the Bermuda butter tasted, and that Mom and I laughed until we were gasping when she said, "We ate all that stinking liver . . . for *this*?"

.   .   .

I don't have an empty coffee can because the one in the fridge is still half full, and I'm making that coffee last as long as possible. But Nathan has a can covered with vintage soda ads that's about the right size, and it makes the same satisfying metallic *clunk!* when a coin hits the bottom.

"What's that for?" Nathan asks when he hears the *clunk!* one morning.

I tell him about how we'd used the coffee can to save for the trip, and then again to put money away to get a new TV set. "A black-and-white Motorola," I say proudly as I put our new can on top of the fridge. "Mom got the floor model at a discount. The thing was huge, and when we got it home she carried it up three flights of stairs herself because she didn't have enough to tip the cab driver to do it."

"Don't you think our extra money would be better off in a bank?" Nathan asks.

"Which one: a bank that's been seized, or maybe one of the banks that's being bailed out?"

"Point taken," he says. "Well, we have a TV, and I'm guessing you don't want to go back to Bermuda. So what are you saving up for?"

"I don't know . . . I hadn't thought about it yet. Maybe a bottle of perfume, or a romantic dinner at a nice restaurant for us. By the time I have enough, we'll figure it out."

I know that Nathan is right; any spare money we have would be better off collecting interest in a bank. But as the days go by, the financial news continues to get worse, and logic be damned—there is something very reassuring about the simplicity of tucking away a dollar here or a nickel there in that can. Mom and I would cheer every time we heard that *clunk!* Today, it just sounds so much better than the yawning, empty silence of my retirement plan.

A few weeks later, Nathan presses sixty dollars into my hand—a tip from a client he did repairs for. 'Put this in the can," he says.

CHICKEN PIE A LA MISSISSIPPI

OLD FASHIONED METHOD

Start with a 4 pound chicken. Cut the chicken up as
you would for frying and simmer the pieces in boiling
water until tender. About 30 minutes before the chicken
is done, add a chopped onion or two. Add a dash of pepper,
a dash of salt, and a little Worcestershire sauce. Leave
the bones in the chicken. When it's tender and in a pan,
add dumplings. Then make a sauce....melted butter and
flour, and about 2 cups of chicken broth. Pour it over
the chicken and dumplings.

For the top, make a good baking-powder biscuit dough,
rolled thin, cut in finger-length strips one inch wide.
When the pie is covered, put it in the oven to brown.

MODERN RECIPE

Start with a 4 pound chicken. Simmer with 1 tablespoon
of salt, 2 stalks of celery and one bay leaf. Add onions,
too. When the simmering is done, bone the chicken and place
in a two quart casserole. Make the sauce of butter and
flour in a double boiler. Add salt, pepper, mace and perhaps sherry wine. Then, instead of strips of dough, cover
the pie with small baking powder biscuits and brush with
top milk or cream. Bake for 20 to 25 minutes, at
450 degrees.

DESPERATE HOUSEWIFE

⤟

Chicken Pie à la Mississippi

OLD FASHIONED METHOD

Start with a 4 pound chicken. Cut the chicken up as you would for frying and simmer the pieces in boiling water until tender. About 30 minutes before the chicken is done, add a chopped onion or two. Add a dash of pepper, a dash of salt, and a little Worcestershire sauce. Leave the bones in the chicken. When it's tender and in a pan, add dumplings. Then make a sauce . . . melted butter and flour, and about 2 cups of chicken broth. Pour it over the chicken and dumplings.

For the top, make a good baking-powder biscuit dough, rolled thin, cut in finger-length strips one inch wide. When the pie is covered, put it in the oven to brown.

*Start with a 4 pound chicken. Simmer with 1 tablespoon
of salt, 2 stalks of celery and one bay leaf. Add onions, too.
When the simmering is done, bone the chicken and place in
a two-quart casserole. Make the sauce of butter and flour in
a double boiler. Add salt, pepper, mace, and perhaps sherry
wine. Then, instead of strips of dough, cover the pie with
small baking powder biscuits and brush with top milk or
cream. Bake for 20 to 25 minutes, at 450 degrees.*

. . .

JANUARY 2008

HUDSON COUNTY, NEW JERSEY

In addition to the recipes Nana wrote down and
collected, I found booklets in the old brown folder.
Famous Recipes in the Philadelphia Manner, for
example, was "Printed in limited edition as a tribute
to all lovers of fine living." It includes directions
for preparing rabbit ragout, shad roe salad, and
Philadelphia hash, and it implores, "Don't call hash
'lowly,' please. It's a dish raised to an aristocratic
level by cookery as it was practiced in early

Philadelphia." We haven't been doing much fine living in the New Jersey manner lately—vacations canceled, restaurants off limits, curtain's down on the theater, the fat lady's sung on the opera . . . So now I'm really looking forward to whipping up some of that hash.

A few of the booklets are promotional materials from food companies: *Fun with Coffee* from the Pan American Coffee Bureau; *Old-Fashioned Eating Pleasure* from Pepperidge Farm; and *Mealtime Magic with California Long White Potatoes*, which features a tantalizing recipe for Potato–Ham Fiesta Cakes. Nana dog-eared the "Winter Salad" page from the *Metropolitan Life Insurance Cookbook*, and she paid thirteen cents for *250 Ways to Prepare Meat* in 1943. Its companion volume, *250 Ways to Prepare Vegetables*, looks less used.

"When we lived on the farm, our vegetables came right out of our garden," Mom says. "We didn't do much to them, just cooked them with a little butter. They were so good—and huge! The tomatoes and the strawberries, especially." Their secret was an old farmer's trick: put the outhouse by the garden. "It sounds disgusting now, but the natural fertilizer made that soil practically atomic," Mom laughs.

Nana also saved a little book called *1003 Helpful Hints and Work Savers to Help You Beat the High Cost of Living*, which was published by the National Newark and Essex Banking Company in 1947. It was written before the postwar boom, when homemakers like my grandmother had to stretch food dollars far, old clothes were mended and kept in as good condition as possible because there wasn't much money for new, and everyone was looking for ways to save on gas, electric, and phone bills. Some of my favorite tips include

#23: *For longer girdle life, fasten garters straight and in the center of the stocking's hem.*

#339: *Stale, dried-up cheese turns into a delicious spread when placed into the meat grinder with chunks of raw onion.*

#924: *It's the rightest kind of thrift to lubricate your car every thousand miles. The friction "gremlins" in your automobile are the little devils that steal the power and waste gasoline, bearings, and other parts in a hundred different ways. This is one case where spending a little saves a lot.*

Aside from the hint about girdle maintenance, this booklet is as relevant for my life today as it was to Nana's over sixty years ago.

My family eventually lived off the fruits and vegetables from the atomically fertile soil in their garden, but Mom tells me that during their first winter in Saratoga, she, Nana, and Grandpa just barely got by on his paycheck from the plant. Nothing could be grown in the winter, and the animals were expensive to feed and keep warm in the barns. Fortunately, the chickens could be eaten after several weeks. "And we ate a lot of chicken," Mom says. "A *loooooooot* of chicken."

Even when Grandpa started selling milk, butter, and eggs to the local distributor, it didn't bring in as much as it cost to run the farm. "Our neighbor, Truman, sold his butter and eggs as specialty items to the hotels in town, so he got more money for them," Mom remembers. "He'd been farming longer, so he had more crops. And in addition to that, he bred collies to make extra money. Your grandpa just didn't know how to do these things, and it was rough up there. Nana had to figure out every way she could to save money."

Lately, I've had to come up with a few of my own hints to help beat the high cost of living. I think they're a little too unorthodox to have made it into Nana's booklet, but she would have understood them.

. . .

#1: Need more money for food and bills? Offer to walk your neighbor's potentially vicious dog.

Arthur lives downstairs from us. He was an adorable bull terrier puppy when his owners saw him in a pet shop about a year ago. The proprietor said Arthur's freshness date was just about up—he was getting too old to sell and was headed back to the puppy mill, and an uncertain fate, if someone didn't buy him soon. It was a great sales pitch, and Arthur was a bargain at seven hundred dollars, marked down from fifteen hundred.

When Arthur started teething, his puppy bites were cute and harmless. Then he got bigger. One night on the way home from work, I ran into Arthur and one of his mommies. "Hey, Arthur, you handsome boy, how aaaa*AAAAARGH!*"

"Arthur, stop that!" his owner said as she pulled on the leash, which made Arthur dig his teeth into my hand a little deeper so he wouldn't lose his grip. "He's just really excited to see you." So excited, in fact, that in addition to trying to eat my hand, Arthur was simultaneously peeing on my suede boots.

"How was work?" Nathan asked when I got upstairs.

"Only slightly less dangerous than home," I said as I wiped off my boot with my dented hand.

That was last year. A week ago we ran into one of Arthur's mommies in the neighborhood, and she mentioned that they were interviewing dog walkers. "How much do they charge?" Nathan asked.

"Twenty-four dollars per forty-five-minute walk," she said. "And we need a walker twice a week for when we work late."

I did a quick calculation in my head—forty-eight extra dollars a week, cash. "I'll do it!" I said, almost peeing with excitement on Arthur.

. .

#2: There's extra cash in your closet—auction off your aerobic shoes!

"I want you to eBay my sneakers."

Nathan looks up from the computer. "You want me to *what*?"

"Put my sneakers on eBay."

He gives me the Mr. Spock raised eyebrow, his logical Vulcan mind once again fascinated by this human he's living with. "What's so special about these sneakers that would make someone want to buy them?"

"They're tush-tightening sneakers," I explain. "And I paid two hundred and fifty dollars for them."

Now both eyebrows are raised. "Okay, let's get these magic tushie sneakers on eBay and see if anyone wants them."

Three days later, we are a week's worth of groceries richer. It's just a shame that we had to sacrifice one bottom line to raise another.

. . .

#3: Why buy pricey water when you can drink for free from the tap? (Just remember to boil it first.)

Bottled water is expensive, not to mention taxing on the planet, what with the fuel to ship it and the plastic to recycle. But we use it because the tap water where we live is questionable.

For Nathan, there is no question. "Don't drink that!" he says if he sees me filling anything from the sink besides the plant watering can. At first I thought he was just being paranoid. We're both native New Yorkers who grew up drinking top-rated tap water and ridiculing everything about New Jersey—until we had to move here after we got priced out of our hometown. Now we boast about our quiet, friendly neighborhood and our cheap, roomy apartment to harried Manhattanites who fret about their living expenses but ask. "How do you even *get* to New Jersey?"

Aside from being the more practical of the two of us, the one who looks before he leaps and sniffs before he drinks, Nathan has lived here longer than I have. He knows that after heavy rains our tap water needs to be boiled due to flooded sewers.

"Can we filter the water?" I asked.

Nathan shook his head. 'It'll probably dissolve the filter."

Now that I'm home, I'm going through a lot of bottled water. I'm one of those people who believes in drinking eight glasses a day, even though I couldn't find a source for that prescription or any evidence to back it up when I researched it for a magazine article. Still, I'm thirsty, and I'm going through our three-gallon jugs of pure mountain spring water too quickly.

It occurs to me one day that we drink our questionable water in tea and coffee—once it's boiled, it's fine. But there's only so much tea I can drink, so when it starts getting cold in the house, I have an idea that kills two birds with one stone: I start drinking boiled tap water to quench my thirst and stay warm. I add a little lemon to mask its taste (which decent water usually doesn't have) and hope that the citrus will kill whatever the high temperatures don't. I'm not sure I'll be able to find any research to prove that, either.

Nathan finds all of this disturbing, and, of course, illogical. "How much water could you possibly need? And if you're cold, why don't you just turn on the heat?" he asks.

"Are you crazy?" I say, perhaps a little harshly. But he knows I'm a thin-blooded person; if I turned up the heat every time I got cold, we'd be living in a tent in the parking space where our truck used to be.

. . .

#4: Save money on gas, parking, and insurance: Get rid of your vehicle.

Four years ago, when Nathan and I were supposed to go on our first date, I was on a fierce deadline. I had a choice of either rescheduling or going to dinner with him and returning to the office afterward to work until midnight. The last time I'd seen Nathan was a week prior, when we'd just returned from the Costa Rican yoga retreat where we'd met. We talked and held hands for the duration of the five-hour flight home. I thought about his quick smile and how easy and good it felt to be with him, and I remembered his handsome face and the sweetness that seemed to radiate from him like a light.

All of these things were the same when we met for dinner the night of my deadline.

"I'll drive you home," he said at the end of an evening of more easy conversation and hand-holding.

"Actually, I have to go back to work," I said. "We're shipping tonight, and I have pages to read."

"Well then, I'll drive you to the office."

He led me to a truck the color of a ripe cherry. He opened the passenger side door for me, and I had to hoist myself up into the cab. The interior was clean, the seats big. A Tweety Bird air freshener hung from the gearshift. The truck was like him: strong, sexy, but with a sense of humor. Nathan drove me back to the office, and we made out like teenagers in the front seat before I went up to the office with blushing cheeks and my hair on crooked.

"Well, *somebody* had a good night," said one of the editors.

On a summer evening two years ago, we drove into the city for dinner at Lombardi's, a pizza joint that's been serving crispy, thin-crust pies in Little Italy since 1905. We were having a deep discussion about what toppings we were going to get on our pizza when Nathan shut the driver's side door of the truck and said, "Oh, crap."

"What?"

He sighed. "I just locked the keys in the truck."

While we waited for the triple-A guy to come with a slim jim, I had a brainstorm. "Be right back," I said. Twenty minutes later I returned with a mushroom and olive pizza and a large bottle of soda. We ate one of the most romantic dinners we've ever had in the flatbed of the truck, watching the line for tables at Lombardi's snake around the block.

For some people, a truck is a convenience for

loading groceries and those bales of toilet paper from the box store. To me. our truck was a two-ton metal scrapbook full of our memories and stories. Last fall, after I got laid off, we drove it to my brother-in-law's house and came home with six thousand dollars to put toward our new health insurance bills. The money we'd save on gas. the garage fee, and having the truck insured and maintained would help out as well.

"It's okay," Nathan said. "You do what you have to do. Besides, the memories aren't in the truck. They're in us."

German Potato Salad

German Potato Salad

4 slices bacon, 1 cup diluted
vinegar, 1/4 cup sugar, 6
good size cooked potatoes,
3 onions.

Cut bacon into small pieces
and brown in frying pan.
Add vinegar and sugar and
allow to cook together until
heated and sugar is dis-
solved. Add to cooked diced
potatoes and diced onions
and allow to heat through.

German Potato Salad

4 slices bacon
1 cup diluted vinegar [½ cup vinegar plus ½ cup water]
¼ cup sugar
6 good-size cooked potatoes, diced
3 onions, diced

*Cut bacon into small pieces and brown in frying pan. Add
vinegar and sugar and allow to cook together until heated
and sugar is dissolved. Add to cooked diced potatoes and
diced onions and allow to heat through.*

. . .

"My wife and I don't get along too well," the barfly slurred at me.

I took his empty glass away but didn't refill it. "You might get along with her better if you spent more time at home instead of here," I said tartly.

I was a terrible bartender. The beers I pulled were all foam, the local strippers hated me because I didn't know they drank two-for-one when they brought in "dates," and I clearly didn't have the sympathetic bartender schtick down. Considering that I was tending bar to make extra money, I was obviously in the wrong business.

But this was during my first recession as an adult, when any job—even the kind I was woefully, horribly unsuited for—was better than none. There was little or no work in my industry, so when my parents announced that they were moving to Miami, I went with them, figuring that I might as well be unemployed in good weather.

There was even less demand for writers in Florida, so I worked as the receptionist in my parents' carpet showroom. Each morning I'd get in my car—the one I'd gotten cheap because the A/C was busted—and arrive at the Miami Design Center a few minutes before nine, just enough time to air out the clothes I'd sweated through and get a café con leche. I catalogued berbers and sisals and answered the phone until five o'clock, when I got back in the Schvitzmobile and drove to the fish shack where I tended bar until midnight. Then I'd drive home, occasionally getting pulled over in ritzy Bal Harbour for going over the 35-mile-per-hour limit. I'd explain to the officers that it was because I was falling asleep and that it was a choice between speeding and a collision. They let me go either because I made sense or they felt sorry for me in my Bloody Mary–stained T-shirt and shorts. At home, I'd make a bowl of spaghetti and pour Cardini's Caesar salad dressing over it, the poor girl's version of fettuccine Alfredo. And I'd fall across my pull-out couch, which I was too tired to pull out, for four or five hours before getting up to do it all over again.

Between shifts I managed to squeeze in a small nervous breakdown, but at least I never had to ask my parents for a dime. I had enough of those in my tip jar.

There's a lot of negativity about being laid off, but I've discovered one of the major benefits: time. More time with Nathan, since I used to get home from work at around eight-thirty on a good night, and now I've got dinner going when he walks in at five-thirty. And more time to make the three-train trip up to see Mom whenever she's got a day off from working at the furniture showroom she runs with Dad. In this economy, when my parents may go half a week without seeing a single customer, Mom and I are spending a lot more time together. Sitting with her at Nana's antique dining table, learning about our history over many cups of tea, is something my old impressive salary couldn't buy.

Mom's got her own stories about heading down south with more hope than money, but they're much happier ones. "It was right around this time of year," she says one night at dinner, "just a few weeks before Thanksgiving, that your Nana reached her breaking point with the farm . . ."

. . .

In a way, Matilda thought as she peeled potatoes by the sink, waiting for Charlie to come home, her husband's impulsive decision to buy the farm had been something of a blessing. If they had stayed in the Bronx, they would have suffered through unemployment and food rationing during World War II. But between the income from Charlie's job at the factory and living on what was essentially a very large victory garden, they'd done better than most.

Which wasn't to say life had been easy—that first winter especially. But Matilda had learned her way around the farmhouse's ancient kitchen thanks to The Grange ladies (who were thrilled with their new hairstyles and makeup), and there was some more income from selling milk, butter, and eggs. Which was also extra work: Charlie had to milk the cows when he got home from a full shift at the plant, and Matilda made the butter herself with a churn operated by a foot pedal. It was exhausting work, but it kept her legs good. She'd swing the milk pail around and around over her head without losing a drop, just as she had with Grandpa's beer pail when she was a kid, to make Carolyn laugh. When the chickens had gotten old enough to lay eggs, they'd started selling those to the distributor too, candling them in the basement and trying to keep them safe from the large, egg-thieving rat that lived down there.

The chickens also provided plenty of meat, if not a lot of variety; Matilda routinely scoured the newspapers and magazines for new variations on the chicken dinner theme. Then they'd had to leave off of it for a while after Carolyn's pet chicken Ferdie, who was born with a peg leg, was accidentally served for a family supper one Sunday.

"Holy Mary Mother of God," Matilda had hissed at Charlie as she held up a drumstick noticeably shorter than the others in the pan.

"Jesus H. Christ!" Charlie had cried as Carolyn howled. "He was with a whole gang of other chickens—how was I to know?"

"For crying out *loud*, didn't you see him trying to limp away from you?"

Matilda now looked over at Carolyn, who was sitting at the kitchen table and keeping her company as she peeled. Her daughter had gotten over the loss of Ferdie after a few weeks of ignoring even the mashed-potato houses her father built for her, the rooftops studded with peas.

Matilda had never been one to shy away from hard work; that wasn't her problem with life on the farm. Adjusting to the isolation had been much more difficult—especially the night she'd woken up to the sound of tires on the gravel driveway.

"Is Daddy home?" Carolyn asked sleepily. She was allowed to sleep with her mother in her parents' bed since Charlie was away nights.

Matilda rubbed her eyes and checked the clock—it was too early for Charlie to be back, unless something was wrong. She looked out the window. Becoming clearer in the pitch-blackness of the country night was a car, its motor turned off and headlights out, coasting up to the house.

"Who's that?" Carolyn whispered, feeling her mother go stiff.

The car sat in the driveway for a few minutes. *Maybe*

they're lost? Matilda wondered. Then two men got out, looked around, and began slowly walking around the house.

The Kallahers had no phone, and the closest neighbor was a mile away.

"*Happy!*" Matilda whispered for the dog. "Happy, where the hell are you? Get out there and bark, you son of a bitch." As she dragged the mutt out from under the bed, she felt his heart thudding and skipping as badly as her own.

There were four entrances to the house: the main and back doors, and two doors in the servants' quarters where the kitchen was. Matilda and Carolyn quickly tiptoed downstairs and began pushing furniture—tables, chairs, a chest of drawers, anything—in front of the doors. There was nothing they could do about the windows. Matilda grabbed a poker from the fireplace and ran with Carolyn to the very back of the house. She hid her shaking daughter under a couch and put her finger to her lips. Then she stood by a window, wielding the poker like a baseball bat as they heard a doorknob rattling.

They stayed there even after the sound of footsteps on the gravel got fainter and the car went away, and they came out only when the sun did. The next day Charlie had a phone installed.

Even that Matilda had been able to get through, but there was a sense of mounting desperation in her now. She remembered first having this feeling when she was ten years old. Riordan had finally married her mother after being forced by a judge to provide for his bastard children—now three in total—and his sisters had found a small apartment for them near the family's brownstone in Jersey City.

"I'm not going, Grandpa," Matilda said.

"You have to, kid," Peter told her. He'd asked Carrie to leave Matilda with him in the Bronx, but the suddenly clan-oriented Riordan had refused. It had taken every ounce of Peter's will not to make Carrie a new widow.

Matilda tried not to cry in front of her grandpa. "I don't want to go with them. I want to stay here, with you." That was it; she started sobbing.

"I know, I know," her grandfather said in his soft German accent, wrapping his big arms around her. "But I'll come visit you all the time. And I'll tell you what, kid: You be a good girl and go quietly, and I'll get you a new bike. What do you say?"

Grandpa was as good as his word, and Matilda

brought her brand-new bicycle with her when she was taken to Jersey City. After one day with her father, Matilda called Grandpa to tell him that the bike was very nice, and if he didn't come and get her she was going to ride it off the top of the building. He arrived the next morning to take her home.

Now Matilda could feel chill air coming in through the window panes, and with it came the same feeling of despair. Soon they'd be in the thick of another Saratoga winter, where the snow fell so hard it could block the door, and Matilda, away from her family for the first time in her life, might go for days without seeing a soul other than her husband and daughter. Living on this farm was too hard, even after all she'd been through. Every day was a struggle, and every night more sadness crept into the house. Charlie's high dreams of being a farmer hadn't panned out, and he'd sit silent in his Morris chair, unavailable to either her or Carolyn, on whom he'd always doted.

Something had to be done. So, after discussing the situation with seven-year-old Carolyn (there was no one else to talk to), Matilda had taken matters into her own hands.

From the window Matilda watched Charlie come

home from work and go to the barn to milk the cows. She saw him run out of the barn a second later and go to the chicken coop; then he sprinted to the house.

"Tillie," he said, "where are the cows and the chickens?"

"Gone," Matilda answered. "I sold them all. The horses too."

Carolyn looked warily from her mother, who never stopped calmly peeling potatoes, to her father, who was likely to explode at any minute.

"Jesus Mary and Joseph," Charlie said in disbelief. "Why would you do such a thing?"

"Because," said Matilda, "I can't take another winter here. We're leaving and going to Florida, and if we don't I don't know what's going to happen."

Charlie looked at his wife for a long moment. Then he walked over to her and put his hand on her shoulder. "Okay" was all he said.

. . .

"And off we went," Mom says.

"What about your dog, Happy?"

"Well, you remember he had that habit of chasing

cars," she says. "One day he just didn't come home, so either he got chased by a car, or he ran off with one of Truman's purebred collies.

"Anyway, your grandfather boarded up the house, and we headed for Florida. We had a hundred dollars for the trip and who knew how long after that to tide us over, so your Nana kept meticulous accounts of what we spent along the way . . ."

OUR TRIP TO FLORIDA

We started off Saturday, November 15th, at 11:30. Stopped at Ballston Library; reached Albany at 1 P.M.

Gas and oil—$2.91. Candy 30 cents.

Lunch in Rensselaer at 1:10. Expense: $1.90

Left 1:30

Stopped Po'keepsie 3:30. Cake 70 cents. Oil 50 cents.

Arrived Midge's [Charlie's daughter Mary, from his first marriage] 5:30. Stayed for a bite to eat. Left at 7:30 for Pop's [Charlie's father, Edmund]. Charlie bought a flashlight— $1.39. Hard candy for trip—69 cents. New black blouse for me—$6.00. We were surprised to see roses still in bloom in Pop's yard. No frost there yet.

OUR TRIP TO FLORIDA

We started off Saturday, November 15th, at 11:30. Stopped at
Ballston Library; reached Albany at 1 P. M.
Gas and oil - $2.91. Candy 30¢.
Lunch in Rensselaer at 1:10. Expense: $1.90
Left 1:30
Stopped Po'keepsie 3:30. Cake 70¢, oil 50¢.
Arrived Midge's 5:30. Stayed for a bite to eat. Left at 7:30 for
Pop's. Charlie bought a flashlight - $1.39. Hard candy for trip -
59¢. New black blouse for me - $1.00. We were surprised to see
roses still in bloom in Pop's yard. No frost there yet.

Sunday, Nov. 16.

Left Pop's at 10:45. Gas and oil - $2.75. Holland tunnel 50¢.
Arrived in Jersey City at 12 o'clock. Hamburgers in Rahway, N. J.
$1.00. Candy & soda 60¢. Passed Bordentown at 2:10. Arrived in
Pennsville, N. J. at 3:45. Weather clear and sunny, but strong
cold wind. Grass here still quite green, and lots of leaves on
trees. Gas and oil $2.25. Took ferry (38¢) and arrived in
Delaware at 4:05. It was a pleasant trip. Arrived in Elkton,
Md. at 4:40. Stopped at a tourist home. Very, very nice.
$5.00 for the night. Went out for supper ($3.75). We asked for
beer and waitress answered 'no beer served on Sunday'.

Monday, Nov. 17.

Left Elkton at 7:40. Went back 7 miles or so to New Castle for
route 13, to Cape Charles, Va. ferry. This is supposed to be a
shorter route than U. S. #1. Time will tell.
Gas and oil - Smyrna, Del. Arrived 9:20. Breakfast $1.15.
$1.62
Temperature 44 - very cold wind.   (Arrived 12:30, left at 1).
$1.90 two gallon can of oil in Montgomery Wards in Pokomoke City,
Md. Also $1.5 in Woolworth's.
Arrived in Princess Anne, Md. at 12 noon. Temperature 52. Clear,
very strong wind. In this territory we especially noticed:
rest rooms signs say for White only. Many colored, especially on
road work. Many flowers, green grass, no frost.
Arrived Cape Charles, Va. at 2:30. Very strong cold wind. Took
Chesapeake Ferry at Cape Charles. S. S. Pocahontas. Trip takes
about 1 hour 45 mins., costs $4.31. Pretty choppy water. Felt
a little green for a few minutes, but it passed. Landed 4:35 at
Little Creek, Va. $1 snack on board.
Gas - Norfolk, Va. Chubby girl attendant says 'come see us again'
Stayed at Scotties' Hotel Court - Norfolk. Very super. Steam heat,
radio, hot water. Supper $3.25. Very good - fried oysters.

Sunday, Nov. 16
Left Pop's at 10:45. Gas and oil—$2.75. Holland tunnel
50 cents.

Mom starts to laugh. "And when we were in the Holland
Tunnel," she says, "the brakes failed. We were driving an
old Model A Ford—I don't know how your grandfather
thought this thing was going to make it from Saratoga to
Miami. And your Nana said, 'Jesus, Charlie, will you slow
down?' not noticing that his foot was on the brake so
hard it was practically going through the floor."

．　．　．

Arrived in Elkton, Md. at 4:40. Stopped at a tourist home.
Very, very nice. $5.00 for the night. Went out for supper
($3.75). We asked for beer and waitress answered "no beer
served on Sunday."

．　．　．

Monday, Nov. 17
Left Elkton at 7:40. Went back 7 miles or so to New Castle for
Route 13, to Cape Charles, Va. ferry. This is supposed to be a
shorter route than U.S. #1. Time will tell.

Gas and oil—$1.62. Smyrna, Del. Arrived 9:20.
Breakfast $1.15.

Arrived in Princess Anne, Md. at 12 noon.
Temperature 52. Clear, very strong wind. In this territory
we especially noticed: rest rooms signs say for White only.

"Coming from New York, we weren't used to that sort
of thing," Mom says. "We couldn't believe it."

. . .

Tuesday, Nov. 18
Left Norfolk at 7:30. Passed through Suffolk, Va. (peanut
center) at 8:15 A.M. Saw first cotton on outskirts of Suffolk.
Breakfast in Edenton, N.C. at 9:40. Delicious. Southern
fried ham n' eggs. Waitress asks "would you-all like
anything else" in the smo-oo-th-est dr-a-w-l. Breakfast
$2.00.

It's a very monotonous ride from Suffolk, Va. to
Jacksonville. Arrived outskirts (6 miles before) Wilmington,
Nc. at 5:15 P.M. Stayed at tourist cabin. Nice cabin, but
chilly. Heated by gas. And no hot water. To make things
more pleasant, it's raining, and Carolyn has a slight cold.
Hope tomorrow is nice.

Cabin—$4.00.

Mom remembers that stretch of the trip well. "Generally, we didn't stop for lunch, just got rolls and cold cuts and ate them in the car as we drove. And this, by the way, was how Nana taught me math: She'd say, 'Okay, we have two dollars for lunch for three people. If baloney costs this much and bread costs that, and you want a piece of candy, how much baloney can we afford?' Leave it to her to turn being broke into a game.

"Anyway, there were leaks in the roof of the car, and it was raining as hard on us inside as it was out. We were laughing so much we almost choked on our sandwiches."

. . .

Wed. Nov. 19
Breakdown outside Myrtle Beach 12:45 P.M. Very desolate road, no houses. Charlie going for tow car.

"Looking back on that now—the wife and child stay behind in the broken-down car on the side of the road . . ." Mom shakes her head and sighs. "That could have turned out very badly. But that's what we did."

Charlie came back with tow car at 1:40. Staying at tourist
cabin. Waiting for car to be fixed.

. . .

Friday, Nov. 21
Yippee! Crossed Florida state line at 4:46.

"We got out and kissed Bessie's old fenders," Mom
says. "The ocean was on one side of the road, and there
were groves of orange trees on the other, and you could
take as many oranges as you wanted. After those barren
winters in Saratoga, being in this place felt like
anything was possible.

"A little while later, we got pulled over by a state
trooper. We thought, *What now?* He took a look at
our license plate and said, 'Do you mean to tell me
that you-all drove here all the way from New York
in *this* car?' Daddy said, 'Yes, sir, we did.' And the
trooper said, 'Well, God bless, and welcome to
Florida.' "

. . .

They moved into a small apartment complex of white
stucco buildings on Biscayne Bay, one block from the

beach. The rent for a studio with a kitchen and a small sleeping alcove was eighteen dollars a week—very reasonable for Miami in November. The owner was a Mrs. Krauser, an elderly lady in a wheelchair whose beautiful daughter lived with her because, as Mrs. Krauser whispered, "She had an unfortunate marriage."

Among their neighbors were the Garretts, whose four children absorbed Carolyn into their fold instantly. They took her to the abandoned naval base at the end of the block, where the buildings were half sunk in the mud. The neighborhood kids were forbidden to go there, so of course that's where they went to play. The Garrett clan also took Carolyn on bottle runs. People moved in and out of the neighborhood all the time according to the season or the availability of work, and the kids would descend on any newly vacant apartments looking for bottles to redeem for candy money. When enough bottles were collected, one of the parents would stand at the corner and watch as the group of children crossed the multiple lanes of Biscayne Boulevard to get to the convenience store on the other side.

Mr. Garrett worked at the local banana packaging plant, and he regularly brought home office supplies.

"Maw," one of the kids would crawl, "can you make us banana and peanut butter sandwiches?" Soon the Kallahers were making their own banana sandwiches with the extras Mr. Garrett dropped off at their door.

On Friday nights Mr. and Mrs. Garrett would take their kids and Carolyn to the drive-in movie theater. There was an extra charge for children, so all the kids would pile in the back, and Mrs. Garrett would throw a blanket over them and tell them to be still and keep quiet—far too great a challenge for the five of them. The ticket taker would see the blanket shaking with fits of giggles, with sounds of *shhh hhh!* and more giggles coming from under it, and say, "Oh, just the two of you? Here you go, have a nice time."

Charlie heard about carpentry work right away, but getting it was another story. Most of the construction jobs in Miami were union run, and he wasn't a member. That left the option of going to a certain corner where men gathered in the hopes of being picked for day labor. Most of them came by themselves, but that first day Charlie drove up in the Model A with Matilda and Carolyn. He got out and walked over to where the men stood, noting the good, sturdy wooden boxes the carpenters had made for their tools. Charlie looked down at the old grain sack he was carrying his tools in, turned around, and went back to the car.

"What's the matter?" Matilda asked.

"I'm never going to get hired," he said. "Look at me." He hoisted the sack.

"They *are* going to pick you," Carolyn said. "Daddy, go back."

Charlie sighed, but he wasn't one to look defeated in front of his seven-year-old daughter. He went back and found a few other guys who had grain sacks, a group of Polish workers who nodded to him in greeting.

Soon a truck drove up, and a woman got out. "I need five workers," she said. "You, you, you two, and you." Charlie was among them, and Matilda had to smile when she saw that the men the forewoman had chosen were the handsomest of the lot.

Even with Charlie's new job, a traditional Thanksgiving dinner was out of the question—money was so tight that a twenty-five-cent raffle ticket to win a twenty-pound turkey with all the trimmings was an extravagance. "But I'm feeling lucky," Matilda said to Carolyn as they headed for the bingo hall to get their ticket.

"That was one of the best Thanksgivings I can remember," Mom says. "It was us and the Garretts and Mrs. Krauser and her daughter—they were the only ones who had an oven big enough for that huge turkey. We all ate together, and then we had enough leftovers to have Thanksgiving dinner for days."

"You got lucky with that raffle," I say.

"That's the truth," Mom says. "We were lucky with the whole trip. When I think of it now—driving down there in that broken-down car with a hundred dollars in our pockets, not knowing where we'd live or what we'd do for money—it sounds crazy. But your grandparents had been through the Depression; what was worse than that? This seemed like a reasonable plan by comparison.

"And you know what?" she says, smiling. "It was warm and beautiful in Miami. Nana had people to talk to, and I had kids next door to play with, and Grandpa worked during the day, came home at a normal time of night instead of at the crack of dawn, and had dinner with us. We were together, and we were so happy."

BUTTER COOKIES

1 stick and ½ of butter
1 and ½ cups of flour
1 egg
1 teaspoon of vanilla
1 cup of light brown sugar
3/4 teaspoon of baking soda
a pinch of salt

Sift the baking soda with the flour and the salt.
Get eggs and sugar and beat until light.
Have butter at room temperature and add to the
eggs and sugar. Add the flour.
You may also add 1/2 cup of coarse walnuts.
Divide into two parts and roll in wax paper.
Keep in freezer overnight.
Slice and bake 10 to 12 minutes.

350°

Makes about 4 dozen.

8

HAPPY WIFE, HAPPY LIFE

Butter Cookies

1 stick and ½ of butter
1 ½ cups of flour
1 egg
1 teaspoon of vanilla
1 cup of light brown sugar
¾ teaspoon of baking soda
A pinch of salt

Sift the baking soda with the flour and the salt. Get
egg and sugar and beat until light. Have butter at room
temperature and add to the egg, sugar, and vanilla. Add
the flour. You may also add ½ cup of coarse walnuts.

Divide into two parts and roll in wax paper. Keep in freezer overnight.

Slice and bake 10 to 12 minutes. 350 degrees. Makes about 4 dozen.

. . .

During our wedding toasts, Nathan's friend Jason took the microphone in one hand and balanced his two-year-old son in the other arm. "Nathan, this advice was shared with me on my wedding day, and now I'll pass it along to you: Happy wife, happy life." Then we cut the wedding cake, and Nathan smushed the piece he was holding all over my face. I licked off the frosting and we went back for seconds.

When the mâitre d' presented me with the top of the wedding cake, Nathan wrinkled his nose. "I'm not sure I'm going to want to celebrate our first year as husband and wife with old, thawed-out cake," he said, so we ate it later that night. The restaurant had given us the leftovers, too, so we ate wedding cake again the next night.

When people said this was the best cake they'd ever had, I knew they weren't just being nice—those layers of airy dark chocolate and sweet vanilla resting on a hazelnut filling and finished with pearly white fondant were incredible. And, like most brides-to-be, I'd been dieting like a crazy person for weeks. After two months of naked salad, steamed vegetables, and plain fish, I think even a cake made out of nuclear orange Circus Peanuts would've tasted divine.

. . .

I was never a picky eater as a kid. Mom remembers that even as a toddler I had a curious palate. "You loved martini olives," she says.

"What were you doing feeding martini olives to a two-year-old?" I ask.

She shrugs. "It was the sixties . . ."

When I was five and discovered that our local Nathan's Famous Hot Dogs stand sold frog's legs—and that they were *really* the legs of frogs—I had to try them. (Yes, they did taste like chicken, probably because they were cooked in the same oil as the chicken, and the French fries, and every other fried item they served.)

Surrounded by good food made by Mom, Grandpa, and Nana, I rarely said no to anything, but I didn't gorge either. I was in tune with my body's rhythms in a way that I envy and miss today: I ate when I was hungry, slowly, tasting the food, humming a little song I'd made up, and pretending I was a giant eating broccoli trees.

My family had no rules about eating. I was never forced to clean my plate, and when I heard the ice cream truck's tinny chimes, Mom would give me a quarter for a strawberry shortcake pop. One of the neighbor mothers would ask, "Isn't that going to spoil her supper?" and Mom would say, "So she'll eat a little later. It's no big deal."

When Nana died, I was suddenly hungry all the time.

. . .

I could tell myself that I'd over-washed my jeans or that the nice man at the dry cleaner had shrunk my skirt, but tight underwear doesn't lie: the truth of the matter was that I'd gained weight. The metabolism that had served me so well had apparently clocked out, exhausted, on my fortieth birthday.

I parked my wide load in a chair at a well-known diet center. I followed their strict eating rules and cut out bread, butter, cookies, pasta, ice cream before dinner, and many other things that make life worth living. Instead I ate mulch.

The results were quick and encouraging, and
I developed little tricks to speed things along, like
eating only salad (without dressing) for dinner the
night before and nothing at all the morning of my
scheduled weigh-in. I watched a woman strip down to
a tank top and gym shorts before she stepped on the
scale and took note: no more heavy jeans and sweaters
for me. From then on, when I got my weekly reading,
I wore only as much as would keep me from getting
arrested for indecent exposure.

And then I met Nathan, whose love of food was
exceeded only by his enthusiastic metabolism, and
who had a nightly habit of eating cookies and milk
while watching hard-hitting news. And he wanted to
share that ritual with me.

I'd known all about the pleasures of eating, and
then the pitfalls. New to me was the romance of it, the
intimacy of having someone break off a steaming hunk
of toasted Italian bread and hand you half, or of
splitting a cupcake, or of being served a croissant with
your morning coffee (complete with full-fat milk).
I reacted to these previously forbidden fruit pies by
devouring them like a starving locust. A few months
of this, and I felt like a chubby locust.

I went back on the weight-loss plan, suddenly declining bread at dinner, and Nathan reacted as though I'd refused to make love: *Not tonight, honey, I'm on a diet.*

One rainy afternoon in April, Nathan wanted to go to a shop on Manhattan's Lower East Side that specializes in exotic flavors of rice pudding with names like Sex & Drugs & Rocky Road. We'd shared our first kiss there the year before, and I could still remember how Nathan's mouth had tasted of cream and oven-roasted cherries.

Now he ordered up a large dish of Coconut Coma while I calculated how many crunches it would take to keep my belly from turning to pudding.

"Let's eat it now," he said.

"Right after lunch?" I asked, stalling. "I thought we'd save it for later, at home, for dessert."

"C'mon, let's have some now."

I was about to argue, but it was ridiculous to have a fight about rice pudding. So I let Nathan feed me a spoonful, and then he handed me a tiny bag. Inside was a jewelry box with my engagement ring.

I had almost messed up his proposal.

The wedding date approached, and now there were dress fittings to think about. I felt schizophrenic in the company cafeteria, bouncing indecisively between the salad bar and the pork tacos. "I can't diet again," I said to one of my coworkers. "I love food too much."

"Of course not," she agreed, because she was the food editor at the magazine. "But then again, you'll be looking at those wedding photos for the rest of your life."

I remembered the single beautiful black-and-white portrait of Aunt Midge and Uncle Eddie on their wedding day, he so handsome in his sailor uniform and she prim and pretty in a suit. A very tiny suit, because at the time Aunt Midge had a nineteen-inch waist.

.   .   .

These days I can make an unemployment check go for miles at the supermarket. I can save even more money by baking. What I can't do right now is diet. I'm already cutting back and counting every penny—I just can't face counting calories too.

"How did Nana stay so slim?" I ask Mom one day as I fold up yet another pair of skinny jeans and put them in the back of the closet.

"She ate half," Mom says.

"Half of what?"

"Anything delicious. If it was a liverwurst sandwich—I know you don't like those, but she loved them—she'd eat half of it. If it was a piece of cake, she'd have half, or just a bite. She'd have one drink, not a couple. She did pretty well that way.

"Also," says Mom, "Nana always said that a thin woman should gain a pound or two every year as she got older to smooth out wrinkles in her face. Besides, she wasn't so skinny. She was a size ten, but she was tall, so she looked curvy."

Gain a pound or two a year? A size ten? All of this is music to my hips. I take out some photos of her, and in them she looks . . . womanly. Satisfied.

That night, on the couch, the news of the day is not so good. But it's buffered by crisp, light butter cookies, which taste especially good when shared with Nathan.

Aunt Nettie's Clam Chowder

Aunt Nettie's Clam Chowder

Aunt Nettie's Clam Chowder

1½ dozen Chowder Clams
¼ lb. Bacon, in one piece
4 large Onions
Bunch curly parsley, celery, leek,
parsnips
3 Carrots
3 Potatoes
Thyme

Clean Clams; cook Parsley, Celery,
Leek, Onions, Parsnips, in enough
water to cover. Add salt. Cook one
hour. Fry bacon in small cubes.
Put Clams, bacon and fat into
water strained off vegetables.
Add thyme. Add large can
tomatoes and diced carrots.

(over)

Then potatoes. Simmer.

9

HOW LONG WILL IT KEEP?

Aunt Nettie's Clam Chowder

1 ½ dozen chowder clams

¼ lb. bacon, in one piece

4 large onions

Bunch curly parsley, celery, leeks, parsnips

3 carrots

3 potatoes

1 large can tomatoes

Thyme

*Clean clams; cook parsley, celery, leeks, onions, parsnips,
in enough water to cover. Add salt. Cook one hour. Fry
bacon in small cubes. Put clams, bacon and fat into water*

strained off vegetables. Add thyme. Add tomatoes and diced carrots. Then potatoes. Simmer.

. . .

"Why'd you throw that away?" I ask Nathan, pointing to the half-eaten banana in the garbage. "Something wrong with it?"

"No," he says with a shrug. "I'd just had enough."

I realize I've crossed over into a bad state of mind when I have to keep myself from turning into his mother and asking him if he's nuts, throwing away perfectly good food like that. With one of us out of a job, the insane cost of health insurance, and my retirement plan and his stocks both practically worthless, who on earth would throw away half a banana? Even though I knew I was overreacting, I could swear I heard Grandpa tsk-ing in solidarity with me, all the way from the sweet hereafter.

Salvaging food is something that my grandfather, Nathan's mother, and anyone who went through the Depression did. In fact, I don't remember anyone in my family throwing away food, either because we ate everything before it spoiled or because there was never so much that it had a chance to go bad in the first place. Occasionally we'd nearly lose something, but Grandpa would refuse to let the patient die. "You just cut the moldy part off the cheese," he d say, wielding his scalpel. "See? It's fine."

"It was *green*," I'd say, all wrinkle-nosed eight-year-old. "I don't want it." As far as I was concerned, eating a piece of cheese that was clearly on its last gasp was one of Grandpa's weird food habits, right up there with chomping on raw potatoes. Whenever he made mashed potatoes (which, since he was Irish, was often), he would take a big bite out of an uncooked spud like it was an apple. "That's what the French call it—*la pomme de terre*," he'd say. " 'The apple of the earth.' That's the way I ate potatoes when I was in France."

"He did that to keep from starving to death during World War I," Mom explains. "And did you know that he, not Nana, was the real cook of the family? She learned to cook when we moved to Saratoga, but he'd been doing most of the cooking before that."

"Wait—how did Grandpa learn to cook?"

"His stepmother," Mom says. "She told him, 'Men should know how to do everything well,' and she taught your grandfather and his brother, George, about the thread count in bed sheets, how to mend clothing, how to select the best cuts of meat, and how to cook. It was good advice, because your grandpa was a bachelor for a while—after he was married . . ."

. . .

APRIL 1915

THE BRONX, NEW YORK

Fifteen-year-old Charlie Kallaher thought his father, Edmund, would be proud to hear that he'd left the military academy to fight in World War I, enlisting with his older brother, George. But Edmund merely sighed with disapproval. "Well, Charles, you've done things your own way."

Charlie was sent to France, where he was shot at and gassed, and on one terrible day he had to amputate a buddy's leg right on the field. Sharp beyond his years and determined to stay alive, he defied a commanding officer who, whether knowingly or not, was ordering his men out of a foxhole and directly into the line of enemy fire. "Over the top, Johnny! Over the top!" he shouted as the men leaped out and were killed, one by one. "Over the top, Johnny!"

"After you," Private Kallaber responded.

"*What* did you say, soldier?" the officer demanded.

"I said 'After you,' *sir.*"

The argument ended when a shell landed nearby. The commanding officer was killed, and the soldiers scattered away from the hail of artillery fire and flying shrapnel. Charlie and his buddies hid from enemy troops in a barn, and in the morning he woke up with rats nestling against his body to stay warm. For food, the men ate potatoes straight out of the dirt.

"You'd think he would have hated eating them raw again, considering the memories that must have brought back," I say to Mom.

She shrugs. "The taste reminded him of how they kept him from going hungry," she says. "That's a good memory."

Charlie came home alive but no longer a kid, having seen too much of the war before he was even of legal age to fight. A few months after his return his girl-friend Molly got pregnant. Edmund was painting trim on the side of the house when Charlie told him he was getting married.

"Well, Charles," Edmund said, his paintbrush evenly skimming the wood, "you've done things your own way again."

"Will you come to the wedding, Pop?"

"I think not," his father said.

The marriage was brief; Molly died of influenza just a few years later. Charles was a war veteran, a widower, and the father of two small children—Charles Jr., nicknamed Chick, and Mary, who was called Midge—all by the time he was twenty-one years old. (No longer a stranger to medical events, he'd delivered both babies himself, at home.) Molly's sisters took the children to live with their families in Connecticut, and Charlie spent the next ten years or so as a bachelor. Able to live quite well on his own with the skills his stepmother had taught him, he felt no hurry to find a new bride.

"Your grandfather was a happy widower for years— it was almost a career with him," says Mom. "When he got the job as a milkman and the Depression hit, not only was he making steady money when nobody else was, but he got to visit all the lonely housewives. He was famous in the dairy company as 'The Heartbreaker of Sheffield Farms' by the time he met your Nana at Orchard Beach in 1930."

The only beach in the Bronx—a stretch of sandy coastline on the east side of Pelham Bay Park—Orchard Beach was packed during the typically hot New York City summers. Matilda was a regular visitor; her uncle Hil was a lifeguard there, as was her boyfriend, Frank, and his friend Charlie.

Frank was crazy about Matilda and desperately wanted to marry her. Unfortunately, his wife back in Germany refused to grant him a divorce. This stalemate opened the door to Matilda accepting an invitation from Charlie to go kayaking from Orchard Beach to Hunters Island one day.

Time passed, the tide rose, and the kayak drifted away, leaving them stranded. Their friend Bruno Hauptmann found the boat and brought it back to them. (A few years later Bruno would be tried and executed for the kidnapping and murder of the Lindbergh baby; Charlie always maintained that his friend had to be innocent.) When Charlie and Tillie, as he called her, got back to Orchard Beach, she told Frank it was over.

"Frank wept hysterically," Mom says. "He was prone to that. For some reason he remained a friend of your nana's, and during the family functions he was invited to, he would either ask Nana to dance and dissolve in tears, or he'd pick me up and cry and say, 'You should have been mine.' Your grandpa would turn red in the face but just look at the floor. He felt guilty."

Tillie and Charlie married, and Chick and Midge, now teenagers, were sent for. Midge arrived with a suitcase full of hand-me-downs from a family that had taken her in more out of obligation than desire. Matilda, who at twenty-one was only a few years older than her new stepdaughter, threw all the old clothes away and immediately took Midge shopping and did her hair. Chick came with some apprehension about this new arrangement, but when he saw how his sister was being treated, he was won over as well.

˙ ˙ ˙

NOVEMBER 1970
THE BRONX, NEW YORK

When he was sixty-eight, Charlie once again became a widower caring for a small child: me.

From the time I was a toddler up until I was thirteen years old, I spent every weekend with my grandparents in the Bronx, and whole summers when school was out. At that time, Nana and Grandpa lived in a middle-class neighborhood in a modest, three-family house at the eastern edge of the Bronx. Long Island Sound was in our backyard, so at high tide we could swim or take the dinghy out for a row, and at low tide there was a nice quarter mile of beach to walk on. It was a safe, close-knit neighborhood with lots of kids for me to play with.

Aside from the obvious benefits for a city child like me, the weekend and summer arrangement worked very well for Mom. She was a devoted mother who worked hard during the week, but when the weekend came, she was still a young, beautiful, single woman who wanted to go out. (And dressed to go out my mother was something to behold. This was the late 1960s and early '70s, so she had the long blond fall cascading around her shoulders, the hot pants, and the boots made more for dancing than for walking.)

After Nana died when I was seven years old, it was just me and Grandpa, and I'd sit on his lap while he wiped tears from his eyes and sang to me:

You are my sunshine, my only sunshine
You make me happy when skies are grey . . .

I was too young to understand the reasons behind his taste for raw potatoes or why he felt the need to save food by any means necessary, and, anyway, he had many more eating habits that met with my approval. He kept big Hershey bars in the fridge, took sweetened condensed milk in his coffee, and always had Entenmann's Crumb Cake on hand. (I routinely pinched all the crumbs off, which drove him crazy, but he never tried to stop me.) He also provided for me and took care of me in a way that I could understand on a simple, almost primal level.

Grandpa was a big, barrel-chested guy with blue eyes and wavy hair the color of iron. He was robust and strong well into his seventies. Mom gave him a fishing captain's hat one Father's Day, and he wore it always, tilted at a rakish angle. My grandfather brought a lawn lounge chair into the living room and parked it by the windows facing the bay, and from this command post he would scan the waters with his binoculars. When he saw a particular type of churning, he'd shout, "The blues are running!" I never saw him move as fast as when a school of bluefish was coming into our part of the sound. He'd run and grab his fishing rod, go tearing downstairs, shout to his friend and landlord, "Ted! Ted, the blues!" and head around the house, down to the concrete patio at the end of the yard. He'd cast his line before he came to a stop, knowing he didn't even have to bait the hook—the bluefish, in a vicious feeding frenzy, would bite down on anything. He'd haul up one for me, one for him, maybe another to freeze; if he hooked another fish before the landlord arrived, he'd give it to him on his way back upstairs. Then the churning school would move on, the whole event taking less than five minutes. My grandpa was the Ernest Hemingway of the Bronx.

He also caught flounder, which was less exciting but just as delicious. And when the tide was low, he'd take me clamming with him. His equipment consisted of a pronged clam rake and a laundry basket with an inner tube around it, which he tied to his middle with a rope. My tools were a diving mask and a toy shovel. We'd wade out until the water was waist-deep on him, which was over my head—I hung on to the floating basket.

"Think this is a good spot, kid?" he'd ask.

"I'm not sure," I'd say, frowning. "Let me check." And I'd take a deep breath, dive down in the murky water, and have at the sand with my pink shovel. If I resurfaced with a clam—"Found 'em!"—Grandpa would start digging, putting the mollusks into the plastic basket. He never took too many, about two dozen or so, but they went a long way. After a successful clamming expedition, I knew we'd be having clam fritters, spaghetti with clam sauce (always red, never white), and his variation on Aunt Nettie's clam chowder recipe. (He wasn't much on parsnips, and he added a bottle of clam juice to the water for flavor and put the clams in at the last stage to keep them tender. I like the parsnips and keep in all the vegetables, and I add about a quarter of a cup of white wine and some salt and pepper.) But Grandpa would use the clams only after keeping them in the vegetable bins at the bottom of the fridge to clean them out, lugging a bucket of fresh seawater upstairs every day for a week.

When I had nightmares, or woke up crying after having a dream about Nana and remembering she was gone, Grandpa would bring his command-post lawn chaise into his bedroom, put it next to the bed, and fix it up for me with my pillow and blankets. "Okay, kid, all set. And I'm right here. Did you say your prayers?"

"I don't know any," I said.

"*What?*" Even in the dark I could see his eyes pop and practically hear him making a mental note to talk to his heathen daughter. His grandchild didn't know the Rosary, or even the "Our Father"? Grandpa was what Mom called a Christmas-and-Easter Catholic, but he still thought I should know at least a few of the usual prayers. "Never mind, I'll teach you. I'll say a line, and you say it back. Ready?"

"Ready!"

" 'Now I lay me down to sleep . . .' "

On Sundays, Mom would come up from the city to get me. First she'd go to Cake Masters and pick up a blackout cake—chocolate cake embedded with cherries and covered with dark chocolate frosting—and a seeded rye, which was put in a big machine that chugged blades down on the bread until it was sliced perfectly. Then she'd take the 6 Train to the end of the line, Pelham Bay in the Bronx, and take a Crosby Cab to the house. We'd all go for a swim or a walk on the beach, and after dinner Grandpa would send us home with quarts of clam chowder and beef stew.

For a child being raised by a young woman who was herself still growing up, and with both of us going through a dark period of mourning for Nana, Grandpa was pure security: a strong substitute father who doted on me and could literally catch dinner in our backyard. As long as I was with him, I thought, nothing in this unpredictable world could hurt me.

* * *

At home in Manhattan I was a fearful kid. Our apartment was on the Upper East Side in Yorkville, not far from where the Guibes had lived before they moved to the Bronx. The neighborhood was great around 86th Street, okay in the upper eighties, and went from dicey to dangerous the further up you went in the nineties. We lived on 89th Street.

Life was occasionally scary, stable only in its instability. A friend from school had a schizophrenic father, and one day the parents were warned to watch out for him because he'd been seen wandering around armed with a hunting knife and a Bible. Another friend was evicted from the apartment she lived in with several relatives newly arrived from China. She had to fight off kids we went to school with as they tried to steal her clothes from the piles the landlord threw out on the street. A boy in my third-grade class told me that a neighbor had been murdered during an attempted robbery: "They beat her up and killed her for a lousy dime," he reported flatly, with none of the childlike glee that would indicate a fib.

On the home front, things were less dramatic but still unsettling. Mom's salary as a secretary/apprentice perfumer at a fragrance company just didn't go that far, and when my biological father missed even one of his sixty-dollar-a-week child support payments, my mother's brow would furrow with worry. The difference between worry and panic was about a hundred and twenty dollars.

One night when I was eight years old, the pin in the old bolt on our door slipped, locking us inside our own apartment. We couldn't call anyone because we didn't have enough money to pay the phone bill that month, so the line was dead. We beat on the door and screamed until a neighbor came and called a locksmith.

I had a series of babysitters who watched me after

school until Mom came home from work. I remember a few lovely ones, like Mrs. Wittick, who kept her support hose up on her swollen legs with rubber bands and read the most violent Bible stories to me as many times as I wished. When I was about nine or ten, old enough to spend the afternoons by myself, I didn't usually play with other kids. I preferred to read or watch Bugs Bunny cartoons while slowly, methodically eating almost an entire Entenmann's fudge cake, square by square. I always saved one last piece for Mom. By the time she got home from a long day at the office, though, she generally needed something a little stronger than cake.

And on Friday nights, thank God and Nana in heaven, I'd be sent back to the Bronx. Grandpa would pay for a cab to bring me there, but not a Manhattan taxi; he had a Crosby Cab come down from the Bronx to get me. He trusted only that band of men who Mom said handled their cabs like getaway car drivers. They smelled of cigarettes and referred to me as "Chollie's gran-*dawtah*," and they were not averse to driving on the sidewalk to cut around a traffic jam. They always got me to Agar Place safely and in record time.

If it had been too cold to fish and get clams, Grandpa

would have beef stew bubbling in the cast-iron pot on the stove, or he'd make hamburgers. He'd get a pound or so of ground meat and roll it out on the cutting board like thick dough and use a tumbler to cut small, perfect burger shapes. He'd serve them with fried onions, two little burgers for each of us, his with a beer. I might even get a shrimp cocktail, the kind that came three to a pack in parfait glasses. We kept those little fancy glasses for my milk, and for my occasional inch of beer.

And the cereal! I had a stash of about five boxes of cereal, which both Nana, when she was alive, and then Grandpa made sure I never ran out of. The idea that there were five boxes of cereal waiting in a cupboard in the Bronx just for me was an incredible comfort.

. . .

DECEMBER 2008
HUDSON COUNTY, NEW JERSEY

One of the most seductive things about my husband-to-be, I remember, was his cupboard.

Nathan had a lot of things going for him: He was handsome, spiritual, intelligent, a great listener, and had a hot yoga body. He seemed like the total package.

After a few weeks of dating, he invited me to his place for dinner. Some men, when having a woman over for the first time, will buy fancy, seductive foods like oysters, pâté, maybe truffles. Nathan wooed me, and won me over, with a stable dinner of salad, pasta, Italian bread, and cookies for dessert.

As I helped him in the kitchen, I took note of his fridge full of eggs, soy milk, yogurt, chicken sausage, cheese, ravioli, and chocolate. He'd get something out of the cupboards and reveal boxes of couscous, many jars of spices, granola, oatmeal, at least seven different kinds of tea . . . He hadn't gone shopping that afternoon because I was coming over—the guy had food on hand. One of the sexiest parts of that meal was knowing there was more where that came from, and maybe always would be.

Breakfast the next morning was even better.

As much as Nathan's full larder reminded me of my grandparents' comfortably stocked kitchen, he differs from members of my family in one major respect: He throws food away. Not just moldy food either. It's like when dinner guests stay a little too late, and Nathan will say, "Well, it's been lovely having you here, and

I hate to say good-bye." Any food that's been hanging around our fridge too long is promptly escorted to the garbage can.

This never bothered me before, but today I can feel myself snapping over half a banana. What next—will I start keeping pieces of string because they might come in handy someday?

I sit there and stare at the garbage can for a while, considering whether I should take the banana out, even though it's been in there long past the five-second rule, but more because I'm wondering how I can get out of this grip of fear. Technically I've only lost my job, but I feel like I'm also losing my footing and the sense that, somehow, everything will be all right. The bad economy causes shifts within my industry to accelerate as more print magazines fold and go online, run by a quarter—a young, tech-savvy quarter—of their former staffs. I worry that I won't be able to make a living as a writer anymore: at forty-five years old, what will be my Plan B? I used to tell my parents they'd never have to worry about their old age, that I would take care of them. Can I say that now?

When I call my mother to say good-night, I lie to

her and tell her things are looking up. She's upset enough watching her own business slowly starving to death; I don't need to add my misery. It occurs to me that my family has been worrying about money for over a hundred years now. This is one tradition I had hoped I wouldn't carry on.

QUICK APPLE CAKE

One egg
One-fourth cup milk
One cup sifted flour
One and one-half teaspoons baking powder
One-half teaspoon salt
One tablespoon sugar
One-fourth cup butter or margarine
Two apples, peeled and sliced
One-fourth cup melted butter or margarine
Two tablespoons sugar
One-half teaspoon cinnamon
One-fourth teaspoon nutmeg
Oven temperature: 400 degrees
Baking time: Twenty five minutes, or more
Servings: Nine

In a small bowl, beat the egg with the milk. Sift together into a second bowl the flour, baking powder,
salt and tablespoon of sugar. Cut the butter or
margarine into the dry ingredients with a pastry
blender or two knives until the mixture is the consistency of cornmeal. Stir in the egg and milk.
Spread batter in a greased pan (8 x 8 x 2 in.)

Press apple slices into batter in rows. Brush top
with part of the melted butter or margarine,
sprinkle with the combined sugar, cinnamon and
nutmeg and top with remaining melted butter or
margarine. Bake in a quick oven until the cake
leaves the sides of the pan and is nicely browned
on top. Serve warm or cool cut in squares.

FINE VASES, CHERRIES IN WINTER, AND OTHER LIFESAVING DEVICES

Quick Apple Cake

1 egg

¼ cup milk

1 cup sifted flour

1½ teaspoons baking powder

½ teaspoon salt

1 tablespoon sugar

*¼ cup butter or margarine [plus about 1 tablespoon,
     melted]*

2 apples, peeled and sliced

2 tablespoons sugar

½ teaspoon cinnamon

¼ teaspoon nutmeg

Preheat oven to 400 degrees. In a small bowl, beat the egg with the milk. Sift together into a second bowl the flour, baking powder, salt and tablespoon of sugar. Cut the butter or margarine into the dry ingredients with a pastry blender or two knives until the mixture is the consistency of cornmeal. Stir in the egg and milk. Spread batter in a greased pan (8 × 8 × 2 in.).

Press apple slices into batter in rows. Brush top with part of the melted butter or margarine, sprinkle with the combined sugar, cinnamon and nutmeg and top with remaining melted butter or margarine. Bake in a quick oven until the cake leaves the sides of the pan and is nicely browned on top, twenty-five minutes or more. Serve warm or cool cut in squares.

. . .

DECEMBER 2008

NEW YORK CITY, NEW YORK

I'm standing in front of Fairway, a high-end market famous for its cheese and olive selection, fresh fish, fine meats, and house-made matzo ball soup, on the Upper West Side of Manhattan. If it's not the Tiffany's of food, it's close. Aside from the high quality of their stock, the location alone adds an extra thirty percent to your grocery bill. The people who live in this neighborhood aren't exactly worried about money, and in the past I would have shopped here without giving it a moment's thought. In fact, being able to do that was one of the signs I'd made good, or as Grandpa would've said, "You've done pretty well for yourself, kid." Today I'll be shopping there with my unemployment debit card.

The only reason I'm going in at all is for the bread and the fish. I was visiting a friend in the neighborhood and walked by Fairway—and almost kept walking because I can't afford to go in there anymore. For a person who loves food, being in Fairway is like being a kid loose in a toy store, and now I was going to tell that kid, "You can have whatever you want, as long as it costs under ten dollars."

But I think about how nice it would be to come home and present Nathan with a loaf of their fine, crusty French bread and for us to have fish—not the kind in our local supermarket that was inexpensive but had been farm-raised, fed pellets, injected with dye to make it look like wild fish, and shipped here from far away. I want *real* fish that has been caught nearby and cleaned before my eyes, almost like the fish my grandfather caught for me. (Now I can add something else to the list of things that show my age: "When I was young, a plain old flounder caught out of the water wasn't a specialty item!") So, seduced by the lure of simple, pure food, I formulate my plan: Get in, get the bread and a cheap piece of fish for dinner, and get out.

The only thing I hadn't counted on was the raisins.

I never thought I could be seduced by a raisin—they're the fruit world's version of sensible shoes—but these are unlike any raisins I've ever seen. The label reads, "French Raisins: No dried fruit of this quality has ever been in New York," and I believe it. Raisins are usually small, dark, dried up, and unremarkable. But these are plump and juicy-looking in a way a normal raisin wouldn't dare to be, still sassy with colors of gold, deep purple, and a full-bodied black. They have joie de vivre.

They're also $5.99 for a small container. Utterly ridiculous. I'm on unemployment and have had practically no freelance assignments or job prospects for weeks. Our heating bills are up. Our health insurance costs almost as much as our rent. I've been cutting laundry dryer sheets in half to make the box last longer, for goodness sake. I should be watching every penny I spend.

At this moment I suddenly feel poor. Not technically, because I have a savings account and a zero balance on my credit card. But this feeling isn't about money. It's why Nana always said, "We may have been broke, but we were never poor." By monetary standards, there have been plenty of times my family came close to the definition of poverty. But now I finally understand what Nana meant.

As I stand there in the market aisle holding the French raisins, I can hear my mother's voice telling me, from the time I was little, the stories of how our family defied poverty not of the wallet but of the soul.

. . .

DECEMBER 1890
NEW YORK CITY, NEW YORK

When Peter arrived home from work, it took him a moment to figure out what was missing: the smell of dinner.

"Matilde?" he called. Little Carrie came running to hug him, holding baby Willie in her arms. He picked them both up, kissed them hello, and went looking for his wife. He found her in the kitchen, but there was nothing cooking on the stove. "Where is our supper?" he asked.

"This is it," she said, nodding toward a loaf of bread and a bowl of cooked apples she was mashing.

"Bread and applesauce?" Peter asked. "But why? I gave you money for food this morning. You said you were going to the market today."

And Matilde had been on her way to the market with her list of what she'd need for the week. She'd had every intention of using the wages Peter earned as a stonemason to buy food for the family. And then she'd seen the vases.

The shop sold fine linens, dishes, silver, and other household goods. Matilde had passed by it many times on her way to the butcher's. If she had a moment, she'd stop and look in the window, and then go on her way. In fact, she'd never even been in the store before—there wasn't any money for pretty, but unnecessary items. But these vases . . .

"Good morning," said the shopkeeper. "May I help you?"

"The blue vases in the window," Matilde said, traces of the French and German territory still lingering on her words. She didn't have to say any more; the man smiled and reached for the vases, carefully putting one on a counter and handing her the other.

Matilde could feel the smoothness of the cobalt glaze on the porcelain through her gloves. She admired the fine detail on the front of the vases, the painted scenes of a lady wearing a high white wig and a billowy dress and a gentleman in uniform, both of them in a garden. Matilde carefully held the small gold-painted handles as she turned the vase over. On the bottom in red ink was a number and the words MADE IN AUSTRIA. Not that far from home. Matilde had been in America for a while, but this smooth, elegant piece had pulled her back to a place she missed too much.

"Beautiful, aren't they?" said the shopkeeper.

. . .

"Yes, they're beautiful! They're lovely!" Peter shouted. "But Matilde, a week's wages? What were you thinking? What are we going to eat?"

Matilde sighed. Her husband's word was law in his home, but tonight she was unrepentant. She ground a little cinnamon on the mashed apples and said, "We have this."

"For a week!" Peter said. "Matilde—"

"We will have these vases long after our stomachs are full again," Matilde said calmly. She pulled herself up to her full, impressive height, picked up a knife, and began carefully slicing the loaf. "So we eat bread and applesauce for a week . . . It will not kill us."

. . .

DECEMBER 1961

NEW YORK CITY, NEW YORK

"Why would you waste so much money on cherries?" Charlie asked Matilda when she presented him with a small cache of winter bings.

"Because," she said, knowing that if she had to explain it, there was no point.

After that, Matilda shared them with her daughter, Carolyn, who understood the importance of a dark red cherry in the middle of winter: the snap of the skin, the tart juice tasting of summers past and the summer to come.

At the time, Matilda was working in the heart of Columbus Circle at the Coliseum convention center— her business cards, which were pink, read MATILDA E. KALLAHER, ADMINISTRATIVE ASSISTANT FOR SALES. Carolyn had just started modeling, and she occasionally worked at Coliseum expos like the auto show. Matilda's boss would look at the teenaged blend of Marilyn Monroe and Grace Kelly and say, "Mrs. K., your daughter should be in college, not draped over a car." But Matilda was convinced that Carolyn was going to be a big star.

Carolyn herself wasn't that hot on modeling, especially after a fortune-teller at one of the Coliseum shows said she was going to die on a photo shoot in Africa at the age of thirty-two. Matilda waved it away. "Just don't go to Africa."

"Okay, but if anything happens to me, promise you'll do my makeup," Carolyn said. "Don't let one of those funeral home cosmeticians do it—they're terrible."

"Same goes for me," Matilda said. "Nobody does my eyebrows but you."

"Deal." They shook on it and went for their regular visit to the fruit vendor around the corner.

For an assignment in her high school creative writing class, Carolyn had written an essay about one of these early evening trips that took place the previous spring. She described her mother as being wistful for Paris, a place she'd never been to and, though they didn't know it at the time, would never see. The indulgence du jour was jumbo-sized prunes, and they ate them out of the paper bag as they walked—something people just didn't do back then. Especially not ladies, whose proper attire included gloves, even in the summertime. As un-done as it was, two blond women almost six feet tall doing it attracted even more attention. Carolyn (who described herself as being the more conventional one) suggested putting the fruit away for later, but Matilda told her not to be silly. "It shows a lot of poise if we can walk along Fifth Avenue eating prunes," she said. Carolyn laughed. "Mother, you are a hobo at heart."

One night in the middle of December, the fruit vendor had the winter cherries. They were pricey all right, but Matilda didn't hesitate. It wasn't that cold out, so mother and daughter walked to the park and sat on a bench to enjoy their extravagance.

"Is there anything better in the world," Matilda said, "than being in Manhattan in Central Park and eating cherries in winter?"

. . .

Matilde gave the fine porcelain vases to Carrie when she got married. Carrie gave them to her daughter, Matilda. And now those vases are sitting on the counter of an antique breakfront in my mother's kitchen.

Nana's winter cherries weren't as expensive as the vases, but they meant the same thing: She spent a little more to keep herself from feeling like less. And when Mom was down to her last twenty and a paycheck wasn't coming until the end of the week, she'd sing, "We need a little Christmas / Right this very minute," and we'd go out for dinner.

We might have Wienerschnitzel at Café Hindenburg, one of ten or so similar restaurants in our neighborhood, which was once called Germantown because of the many German immigrants who settled there, including Nana's grandfather Peter. Or we'd go to the Flaming Embers for a $4.99 steak-and-potato dinner. We might even get a cherry pie, which we'd take home and eat, bite by bite, over the next few days.

The women in my family have certain traits: height, prominent noses, and the ability to rationalize spending extra, just once in a while, when there is no extra to be spent. *Because*. I got some of their height and all of the nose, but I thought that last characteristic was missing in me. It wasn't; I just didn't realize that it only wakes up when we begin to measure ourselves by money, or the lack of it. It's not a reflexive kick of denial about having less. It's a deep breath reminding us not to become miserly in spirit. We may be broke, but we're not poor.

The French raisins are a revelation. They look and taste like jewels. Nana would have loved them.

WHAT PRICE BEAUTY?

YOUR MAKEUP AT WORK: Dewy. Natural eyebrows, and if penciled, carefully, carefully—never obviously. If you use eyeliner, only on upper lid, never lower. Never go without lipstick; it only makes you look washed out. Nothing looks better than a slightly rosy red mouth.

HOW YOU SMELL AT WORK: No perfume—ever. Baby oil and talcum powder for you. Delicious.

From "You've Got to Be a Bitch to Get Ahead!"
by Matilda Kallaher

. . .

Nana was a showstopper. She fit the stereotypical grandma profile in only one respect: her white hair. But she wore it stylishly short, with a Marilyn Monroe wave swooping down over one eye. She was incredibly chic—one of the first things people said about her, and still do, is how elegant she was. You'd never know she came from a family so perpetually broke she'd nearly starved to death, and that was the point.

When I was five I wanted to be fifty-five so I could look like Nana. She would let me wear her dresses and her jewelry, and I couldn't wait for the day my hair would turn white like hers. She wasn't a beauty—that was my mother, and even as a kid I sensed I'd never be as traffic-stoppingly gorgeous as Mom was. What Nana had was more attainable: a sense of style. She'd taken what she had and made the most of it.

She started with fine manners. "If you want to get along with everybody at a cocktail party," she told my mother, "don't discuss sex, politics, or religion." (Unless a party was dull, that is; then she'd take gentle swipes at both politics *and* religion. "When all else fails," she told Mom, "kick the chandelier.") Then she dressed impeccably, though she never owned expensive clothes. She took note of what was in fashion and found something similar for less money at bargain department stores like Loehmann's and Alexander s, or she stuck with classics and let inexpensive costume jewelry reflect the current trend. Last and most important, Nana made sure everything she wore fit her hourglass figure perfectly.

After a trip to Alexander's, she'd stop at Papaya King, a hot dog stand, for two dogs with mustard and sauerkraut and a papaya drink. Then she would treat herself to a taxi home. ("She saved money on clothes and food, but she lived rich," says my godmother Barbara.)

After she turned fifty, Nana wouldn't wear black scarves or tops: "It drains the life out of a woman's face," she said. She never, ever went anywhere without her lipstick (shocking pink was her color), advice she shared with young secretaries in that article she wrote in the 1960s called "You've Got to Be a Bitch to Get Ahead!" She did her manicures herself, and she always cut her own hair.

. . .

I used to get my hair cut by a stylist—once they start using that title instead of "hairdresser" they're charging serious cash, and this one was no exception. She billed three hundred dollars for a cut, and I never would have gone to her if I'd had to pay that much money. But I got a discount for having been a loyal customer since the days when her fee was a mere two hundred, and another because I put in a good word for her with beauty editors in the magazine industry. My defense for the still-high expenditure was that with my curly/wavy/frizzy hair I needed an expert. Also, I saved money on hair color since I was letting my grays come in, hoping to fulfill my childhood dream of having hair like Nana's.

I got no such discounts on skincare products, but I had sensitive skin that needed two special cleansers, one with pineapple and papaya for morning, and a creamy one for evening, along with an oil-free moisturizer for summer and a heavier one for winter. After that, what was another seventeen dollars for a good, alcohol-free toner?

My signature scent was an eau de toilette that goes for a relatively inexpensive fifty bucks per ounce. I changed it a few summers ago, and one day Nathan hugged me and suddenly looked sad. "I didn't recognize you," he said. "You smell different." I ran back to the perfume counter and bought two bottles of the old fragrance.

Every six weeks or so was Eyebrow Day at the magazine, when an expert would come into the office to tweeze and shape our brows. As with most questionable indulgences, the first taste was free, but after that I cheerfully handed over forty dollars every time the plucker lady came to visit.

During especially hectic deadline weeks, I might treat myself to a massage at the health club that was very conveniently located in our office building.

Doing these things, and having the money to do them in the first place made me feel like I'd arrived. But there was a limit; I always did my own pedicures. I didn't see the point in spending twenty bucks at the salon when I did a better job myself.

. . .

DECEMBER 2008

HUDSON COUNTY, NEW JERSEY

Just as my eating habits changed when I stopped having lunch in the company cafeteria, my beauty routine has been modified somewhat now that I'm self-employed (which sounds so much better than *un*employed). In December I had one last salon hurrah with a hairdresser—note title change—who charged half of what my old stylist did even after my discounts. These days I wait until I get the five-dollars-off coupon at the drugstore before I buy my new, cheap skincare products, which, to my surprise and chagrin, work just as well as the expensive stuff. (Mom is also cutting back wherever she can, but she's not going along with me on this one: "I'd rather go without food than my face cream.") Every other week or so is Eyebrow Day at my home office, where I pluck anything that strays outside of what I remember the expert's outline was for my brows. I have bangs now, so no one can see them anyway if I make a mistake. I still make appointments for massages, and they're very conveniently located in my building—right on our couch. While Nathan watches *Frontline,* he'll grab my home-pedicured feet and knead my arches and toes for a while. It's heavenly, and far more pleasurable than being Rolfed by a stranger.

Unfortunately, my hair is getting shaggy right around the same time that my cat Tootsie's teeth are about to rot right out of her head.

In the past, these two events would have been completely unrelated. Now, with things being what they are, I can make an appointment with my hairdresser, or I can make an appointment with my veterinarian. But I feel like I can't afford both.

(I pause here for a moment for a perspective check. There are a lot of people who can't afford to get their *own* teeth fixed right now, much less their animals'. I feel very fortunate that we have enough money to keep all the teeth in our house, whether human or feline, present and accounted for.)

Of course, there's no decision to be made. I'd give up my hair appointments forever and become the Wild Woman of Borneo before I'd let my cat be in pain or even have to forgo the crunchy kibble she likes so much. Nor will I repurpose my monthly donations to the ASPCA and the local food bank for this expense. I've had to cut down on the amount I give, but I refuse to cut charitable donations out completely. There have been too many stories of pets left behind in abandoned homes and last year's food bank donors becoming this year's recipients. Not giving while I still have something to give, no matter how little, is an inner beauty routine I won't do without.

Besides, I know a hairdresser in Westchester who can give me a decent, simple bob. She's been cutting her own hair for a long time, as did her mother before her. And after she cuts my hair, she'll even make us some lunch and tell me another story about my family.

Oh, and the perfume? I've been rationing the last of the bottle I have, unable to bring myself to spend money that might be needed elsewhere. In its place I started using Nana's suggested combination of baby oil and talcum powder and hoped that Nathan would still recognize me.

One night when we were about to fall asleep, he put his head on my chest and sighed. "You smell amazing," he said.

Beef stew with yeast dumplings

1/2 cup flour
1-1/2 tsp. salt
1/4 tsp. pepper
2 pounds beef, cubed
3 tbsp. shortening
1 bay leaf
1 clove garlic (optional)
1 pound small white onions
6 carrots, cut into large pieces
3 med. potatoes, halves
1 package frozen peas or cut beans
1 receipt yeast duplings (see below)

1. Mix flour, salt and pepper in a pie pan and coat each beef piece
    of beef with it.

2. Heat shortening in a heavy pot or Dutch oven, add enough of the
    floured meat to cover the bottom and brown the meat well over
    moderate heat. Remove, if necessary, to brown remaining meat.

3. Return all meat to the pot and add water to cover, bay leaf and
    garlic. Bring to a boil, lower heat, cover and simmer slowly
    until the meat is almost tender, or about two hours.

4. Add onions, carrots and potatoes and cook for ten minutes. Add
    peas or beans. If the stew is to be served without the dumplings,
    continue simmering until the meat and vegetables are tender, or
    about 20 minutes.

5. The yeast dumpling batter will take about thirty minutes to rise
    and should be prepared about half an hour before the vegetables
    are added. Add dumplings and finish stew as directed below.

Serves six.

Yeast dumplings

1 pkg. active dry yeast - 1/2 cup warm water - 2 tbsp. sugar - 3/4
tsp. salt - 1 tbsp. salad oil, 1 tbsp. minced onion, 1 egg, beaten,
1-1/2 cups sifted flour.

1. Soften yeast in water. Add remaining ingredients and stir until
smooth, or about one minute. Let rise in a warm place, such as a pan
of warm water, until double in bulk, or about 30 minutes.

2. Stir down and drop by tbsps. on the simmering stew, letting the
batter rest on the meat and vegetables. Cover tightly and steam
dumplings for 20 minutes without raising cover.

FORECAST: BLEAK TODAY, CHANCE OF THE UNIVERSE PROVIDING TOMORROW

Beef Stew with Yeast Dumplings

½ cup flour

1 ½ tsp. salt

¼ tsp. pepper

2 pounds beef, cubed

3 tsp. shortening

1 bay leaf

1 clove garlic (optional)

1 pound small white onions

6 carrots, cut into large pieces

3 medium potatoes, halved

1 package frozen peas or cut beans

Mix flour, salt, and pepper in a pie pan and coat each piece of beef with it. Heat shortening in a heavy pot or Dutch oven, add enough of the floured meat to cover the bottom and brown the meat well over moderate heat. Remove, if necessary, to brown remaining meat. Return all meat to the pot and add water to cover, bay leaf, and garlic. Bring to a boil, lower heat, cover and simmer slowly until the meat is almost tender, or about two hours.

Add onions, carrots, and potatoes and cook for ten minutes. Add peas or beans. If the stew is to be served without the dumplings, continue simmering until the meat and vegetables are tender, or about 20 minutes.

The yeast dumpling batter will take about 30 minutes to rise and should be prepared about half an hour before the vegetables are added. Add dumplings and finish stew as directed below. Serves six.

Yeast Dumplings

1 pkg. active dry yeast
½ cup warm water
2 tbsp. sugar
¼ tsp. salt
1 tbsp. salad oil

1 tbsp. minced onion

1 egg, beaten

1½ cups sifted flour

Soften yeast in water. Add remaining ingredients and stir
until smooth, or about one minute. Let rise in a warm
place, such as a pan of warm water, until double in bulk,
or about 30 minutes.

Stir down and drop by tablespoons onto the simmering
stew, letting the batter rest on the meat and vegetables.
Cover tightly and steam dumplings for 20 minutes without
raising cover.

•   •   •

DECEMBER 2008

HUDSON COUNTY, NEW JERSEY

In a heavy-handed twist to the plotline, the recession
really kicks in just in time for winter, and both the
stock market and the temperature begin to plunge
simultaneously. Both of these chilling developments
are an excellent reason to start cooking up a hearty
(and inexpensive) beef stew.

My grandparents used their big black Dutch oven to

make stew; my mother still has it, and I think it's at least fifty years old, if not more. "It's a well-seasoned pot," she says with admiration. I'll have to settle for our Crock-Pot, which may be only about five years old, but I'm looking forward to seasoning it with one of Nana's old recipes.

. . .

Last summer Nathan installed Wi-Fi in our apartment. "Now you can go online anywhere in the house," he said. I could if I had a new computer; mine was over seven years old, which, from a technological point of view, put it on the level of an arrowhead. It didn't matter, though, because when I needed to go online, I had my computer at work. Until I didn't.

Coincidentally, I'd bought that laptop when I'd been laid off during the last recession, in 2001. I still had a part-time job at another magazine then, so buying a new computer didn't seem like such a big deal. Besides, to a writer a working computer is as essential as a nice sharp arrowhead was to a hunter.

This time, though, the idea of spending a couple of grand on anything, even the lifeblood of a freelance writer, is scary. I no longer think about money in numerical amounts but in terms of what it means to us: *That's a month's rent and four weeks' worth of groceries!* I decide to make do with the computer I have. Unfortunately, it's heading into its final winter and starts dying on me.

Our apartment has an upstairs full of windows where the living room, dining area, and kitchen are. It gets sunny and warm, and it's perfectly suited for writing—if your laptop can pick up Wi-Fi at more than three inches away from the modem. If not, you have to plug directly into the modem in the office, which is downstairs, doesn't get direct sunlight, and is at least ten degrees colder than it is upstairs. You can actually feel the temperature zones dropping as you descend the spiral staircase.

Our electric bills were reasonable when we were using lights and heat only at night and on weekends. Now I'm home all day and afraid of the numbers we'll rack up if I turn anything on for more than a few minutes. In a magazine I see a photo of a family sitting at the dinner table while wearing their down parkas. At one time that might have been shocking, but now it makes perfect sense to me.

On days when it's bitter outside and oppressively

nippy in my little home office, I take a cue from the parka family and bundle up—two pairs of thick woolen socks, a long-sleeved T-shirt with a turtleneck over it, and a cashmere sweater over that. (The irony of wearing an expensive sweater while being afraid of what the heat would cost wasn't lost on me. I should have gone all the way and worn pearls.)

I roll up the shades and get enough sunlight to work by, but days that it rains and snows are the worst, cold and dark. I had always liked rainy and snowy days, but now they depress me.

"We hated them too," Mom tells me one day when the chill drives me upstairs for a morale-boosting phone call. "When we moved back up to Saratoga from Florida, your grandpa was in construction. It brought in decent money, but they were working high up—twenty stories, sometimes—and if it rained or snowed, they wouldn't let the workers go up. Too dangerous."

The men only got paid when they were on the job. Bad weather meant no work, and that meant no wages for the week. Because Charlie and Matilda were living hand-to-mouth, a period of stormy weather meant trouble. "People always say, 'Oh, the snow is so pretty,' " Mom says in a saccharine tone. "Well, it scared us. I still hate snow."

. . .

Right around the time I discover how hard it is to reboot a computer while wearing fingerless gloves, the laptop struggles back to life and dings feebly that I have a new e-mail: *Please come to the office to pick up your Mr. Crump check.*

Oh my God. I got a Mr. Crump check.

The legend goes that when the namesake of our company was just starting out and the holidays came along, she realized she didn't have enough money for Christmas. Just as she was about to send apologies instead of gifts to her family, her boss, Mr. Crump, announced that he was handing out bonuses to all the employees. Then and there our leader-to-be made a vow: if she ever became a boss and had the means, she'd give her staff bonuses in December in honor of Mr. Crump's generosity. And even though I'd been laid off a few months ago, my Mr. Crump check was at my old office, waiting for me. A check that would pay for a new Wi-Fi-capable laptop computer.

When I tell Mom the good news, she's pleased, but not all that surprised. "That's not the first time money's come out of the blue when it was least expected and most needed," she says. "Remember Nana's black coat?"

.   .   .

It wasn't long after Nana died, suddenly and unexpectedly one night in November 1970, that Mom got fired. She'd been doing well at the perfume company, but when she took off more than the three days allowed for mourning, her boss said, "I needed you here, and I'm sorry you weren't happy with us." The severance check kept us afloat for a while, but that, and the money from Nana's insurance policy, eventually ran out.

Aching for her mother, Mom put on Nana's black faux-lamb coat one night and wrapped it around herself like a hug. "I don't know what we're going to do," she said, the words becoming more like howls as she sobbed. She put her hand in the pocket of the coat. "I don't know how—"

She stopped talking, and when she pulled her hand out of the pocket she was holding a bankbook with a wad of bills folded in the middle. Five hundred dollars in cash, twenty-five hundred in the account. Nana had never mentioned her secret stash to Mom, but she sent it to us just when we needed it the most.

.   .   .

Upstairs the warm, comforting aroma of beef stew fills the kitchen, and the winter sun is so bright it's making me squint. But I won't move, even though this new computer can go anywhere in the house and do practically anything a writer could ever need it to do.

$5 DAILY FOR FAVORITE RECIPE

Chicken Roman

One tender capon (5 lbs.) disjointed

One cup vegetable shortening, melted

One loaf bread (16 oz.) dried, crust removed, grated

One cup grated Parmesan cheese

One-fourth cup minced parsley

One-eighth teaspoon paprika

One-eighth teaspoon pepper

One-half tablespoon salt

Two cloves garlic, minced

Oven temperature: 350 degrees

Baking time: One and one-half hours

Servings: Six

Have the capon disjointed in the market. Wash; dry. Melt the shortening in a saucepan. Dip each piece of chicken into the shortening then into the grated bread mixed in a pan with the cheese, parsley, seasonings and garlic. Place in a large baking pan. Bake in a moderate oven until a golden brown, turning several times. Serve hot with mashed potatoes and stewed tomatoes.

13

A TEN-DOLLAR BET AND A
FIVE-DOLLAR WINNER

Chicken Roman

One tender capon (5 lbs.) disjointed
One cup vegetable shortening, melted
One loaf bread (16 oz.) dried, crust removed, grated
One cup grated Parmesan cheese
One-fourth cup minced parsley
One-eighth teaspoon paprika
One-eighth teaspoon pepper
One-half tablespoon salt
Two cloves garlic, minced

Oven temperature: 350 degrees
Baking time: One and one-half hours

Servings: Six

*Have the capon disjointed in the market. Wash; dry. Melt
the shortening in a saucepan. Dip each piece of chicken
into the shortening then into the grated bread mixed in a
pan with the cheese, parsley, seasonings and garlic. Place
in a large baking pan. Bake in a moderate oven until a
golden brown, turning several times. Serve hot with mashed
potatoes and stewed tomatoes.*

JANUARY 2009

HUDSON COUNTY, NEW JERSEY

"Okay, hold still and don't breathe," says the technician as she sprints to the computer that runs the
mammogram machine.

With a breast clamped firmly in a plastic vise,
there's not a lot of moving I can do, and breathing is
limited to the gasp I sucked in when the technician
pulled skin from my back to get enough flesh to put on
the machine. (I have the same slight bust that Nana had,
while Mom got all the va-va-va-*voom* in the family.)

While I wait those interminable, still, breathless
seconds for the mammogram to be taken, I think about

the core biopsy I had a few years ago. "If you take any more pictures, my boob is going to glow in the dark," I told the doctor.

"We found something," she said. "We're just making sure before we schedule the procedure." After that she didn't have to remind me to hold my breath

The biopsy was relatively simple—a morning in the doctor's office, a lot of local anesthesia and pressure from the needle, and I was even allowed to breathe. "You're doing fine," the nurse said. "But there's a lady in the waiting room who looks like she's going to pass out." Dealing with Mom's anxiety over my biopsy was far more difficult than the surgery itself.

Her fear that I would be the first member of the family to have cancer was fueled by old memories from when she was fifteen and her mother had to go into the hospital for a biopsy. Nana hadn't handled the news well. She was so convinced the procedure would become a mastectomy that she bet the doctor ten dollars she'd wake up without her breast.

After the operation, the doctor laughed when he told her that she'd called his ethics into question by talking about the wager as she came out of the anesthesia. She forced him to take her money when he gave her a diagnosis of benign cysts, saying it was the best ten dollars she'd ever spent.

"How many more?" I ask the technician.

"Only four more images to go," she says. "Just to make sure."

.   .   .

When I'm done with the mammogram, I make my ten-dollar copayment, grateful for our health insurance, and come home with an aching chest and an empty stomach—never a good combination. My evening appointment meant there was no doctor on duty to give me a preliminary reading, so now I get to wonder for the weekend.

I need a distraction, and tonight it comes in the form of making Chicken Roman, one of the $5 DAILY FOR FAVORITE RECIPE winners among Nana's newspaper clippings. There's no date on the recipe, but I can tell it's pretty old because it calls for dipping the bird in melted shortening. I hope I'm not affecting the authenticity of the creation by using a beaten egg, but we ran out of shortening in the early 1970s.

After that, I coat the chicken pieces in a mixture of store-bought breadcrumbs (my lazy substitution for

"one loaf bread, dried, crust removed, grated"),
Parmesan cheese, parsley, minced garlic, salt, and
pepper. I don't notice until all of this is done that the
baking time is an hour and a half in a "moderate oven,"
and I'm starving. So I set the oven to an immoderate
425 degrees, put the roasting pan in, and look up
chicken cooking times on the Internet. I don't want to
see a second doctor tonight because I've given myself
Chicken Romanosis, but I'm hungry and edgy.

Nathan is on the couch, either asleep or passed
out from hunger. This is good, because most of the
cooking times for chicken on the Web say to keep it
in a 350-degree oven for at least 45 minutes. A few
recommend an hour to be on the safe side. I wonder
if boosting the temperature to 475 degrees will cut
the cooking time. I wonder whether I'd be playing
chicken roulette if we didn't still have health insurance. I wonder about my breasts. I watch Nathan
napping peacefully and remember the time he came
home from work with a second-degree burn on his
hand after a blowtorch he was holding slipped. The
chicken cooks a little longer as I wonder what we'll do
when my COBRA runs out and we either have to dial
down our medical plan or come up with more money.

I remember Mom, pale and frightened after my biopsy procedure, and Nana being convinced she was dying. And then I decide to slow down.

There's a lot to be said for not knowing. It's a pause during which I get to choose how I spend my time until I get an answer. Now, give me a solid reason to be scared, and I'll lose my thin coating of composure faster than any chicken. I'd been fairly steady until the oncologist told my beautiful friend Marnie there was nothing more they could do for her. Then I held her hand for my own comfort as much as hers, and I rarely let go until the night she took her last, long breath.

I don't blame Nana for having been afraid, and I love Mom for being afraid for me. But I'm surprised at how these two women, both so strong, could fall apart over a possibility when their realities were so often downright scary.

In my family, trying to avoid some sort of bad time was, as Mom puts it, "Like running through rain-drops"—we were going to get wet no matter what. Good health has always been the limbo stick under which negativity must try to pass. If a boyfriend broke up with me, Mom would say, "Listen, at least you have your health." When I was particularly whiny about some disappointment or another, she'd pull out her tough-love variation on the theme: "Look, you have all your teeth, don't you? All of Nana's front teeth had to be pulled because she was malnourished during the Depression!" It was true; she wore a bridge, and the tooth story always shut me up quick.

Nana had seen wars come and go and the stock market go up, come crashing down, and climb again. She'd never had much money, so the idea of being perpetually broke never fazed her. But just the thought of being ill undid her. This is the first chink I've ever seen in her shocking pink armor, and the first time I have aspired to be different from my Nana. Until I have something to be scared of, I'd rather turn the chicken down, have a piece of bread and cheese to tide me over, and watch my husband's chest rise, fall, and rise again.

An hour later Nathan and I agree that Chicken Roman absolutely deserved its five-dollar award. And a week later I get the results of my mammogram: all clear. Ten dollars well spent.

14

WE WISH YOU A MERRY TUESDAY

I wish when my daughter was little, someone had spoken to me as I am trying to speak to you now. The time goes too fast. If your children are small, enjoy them as much as possible. They need and want your company now. Never again in their lives will you be so close and so important to them. Color with them, or make small clay animals—but you do it, too. Don't just give them a batch of toys and say: "There you are—now go play; mother's busy." I think just the way a child looks at you when you get down on the floor with him or her is a wonderful experience. Watch the little crooked smile you get.

From "Time Out" by Matilda Kallaher

. . .

My husband is a spiritual man who feels, as Nana,
Mom, and I do, that his faith is too large to be
contained or defined by any one formal religion. But
if he were to convert, he would most likely become a
Jehovah's Witness. "They don't celebrate birthdays,
Christmas, Valentine's Day, anniversaries, or any
other forced-affection holidays when, if you don't
buy someone a present, you're in trouble," he
declares.

So, although I've never received a gift from
Nathan in December, he has come home on a random,
garden-variety Tuesday, when the calendar is
free of red ink reminding us of some major event
or other, and presented me with a black pearl
suspended from a clasp studded with tiny diamonds.
He'd prefer for me to know that he loves me every
day, not just the day that I, or even Jesus, was born.

. . .

Nana set out the milk and cookies for Santa. "You have to go to bed, or he won't come in," she said, shooing me off to the pullout convertible bed we slept on.

"How's he going to get in here, anyway?" I asked. I was looking at my grandparents' mantelpiece, which housed a wonderful fake fireplace—tinfoil crunched on a rotating rod, with a small lightbulb that shone behind a red plastic "ember" in the center of a bunch of "logs." I would stare at the "fire" as mesmerized as if it were real, but tonight it presented a problem: There was no actual chimney for Santa to come down, just a small hole at the back for the electric wire to go through. "He's not gonna make it," I said doubtfully. "Maybe we should wait up and let him in—"

"Santa's smart," Nana said. "He'll figure out a way—but not if he sees you awake. Come on, let's get to sleep."

In the morning, my five-year-old jaw dropped at the sight of a half-eaten cookie and an empty milk glass on the kitchen table. Next to those was a note:

It was delicious. Thank you—S. Claus.

"He was *here*!" I gasped at Nana, who just nodded.

But Christmas wasn't the only special day at my grandparents' house. Nana always figured out a way to mark the occasion of my just being there, or of my just being. She made houses out of sheets and chairs— something she'd done when Mom was little—and she'd crawl under them with me. Lunches were always fancy tea parties where she served our food on special doll plates and we wore her long satin gloves. For someone who hadn't been played with much as a child, she knew how to show a kid a good time.

Every time I was with Nana was special. Or maybe every time I was with her, she made me feel special.

. . .

JANUARY 2009

HUDSON COUNTY, NEW JERSEY

"I can stop by the market on the way home from work," Nathan says. "Do we need anything?"

"Just some fish for dinner. Nothing else. We don't need anything else, okay?" I hate my false tone of assurance that everything we could possibly want or need is already in our fridge; it's just a ploy to keep Nathan from spending money on the former necessities that are now luxuries.

An hour later, Nathan comes home with the fish—two thick slices of Chilean sea bass, certified sustainable, which made it politically correct and added a few dollars to the cost of each already expensive piece. He also pulls out a half pound of fresh shrimp; a bottle of pink fizzy *limonade*, imported from France; an artisanal cheese; not one but two containers of olives; and a box of truffles—organic, no less. At the bottom of the cloth shopping tote was the receipt: nearly seventy dollars, for one dinner at home.

"The truffles were on sale," he says cheerfully, kissing me on my suddenly pale cheek.

I've made it a practice never to look a gift horse in the mouth, especially when it brings me food. Horrified at the price of our dinner, I run downstairs and make love to my husband immediately. Then I free myself from pointless fretting about money that's already been spent with a simple rationalization: Christmas can be any night—like tonight.

In the past few months I've learned a lot from Nana, and one of the most important lessons is acting on the knowledge that time spent with people we love is the best gift; the catch is that it's temporary. There was no warning before Nana died. We thought we were going to see her that weekend. One night she was in the bathroom, setting her hair, getting that lovely swoop over her eyes just so. Then Grandpa called us to say that she was gone. Being seven years old, I didn't understand what an aneurysm was. I only knew that people—no matter how important they were to me—could disappear in a second. Every day I'd spent with her became incredibly meaningful in retrospect, since I now knew that there were no more to come.

So tonight, an ordinary Tuesday, I start preparing not a dinner, but a party. I carefully arrange the shrimp in patterns on the salad. I place the olives—plump purple beauties and sharp Greek cured black ones—in a special ceramic dish. The Drunken Goat cheese, aged over sixty days but still stark white against its plum-colored rind, goes on the good china, along with warmed Italian bread. I broil the sea bass with a touch of butter, salt, and pepper until the skin is crispy. After dinner, we try the truffles, dark lumps of cocoa-dusted cream that send the mouth, and the spirit, into ecstasies as they melt and disappear.

We fill our glasses with the tart French lemonade and toast the fact that we are here, together. That's reason enough for a celebration.

Lemon Meringue Pie

5 eggs, separated
1½ cups sugar
1 tbsp. grated lemon rind
¼ cup lemon juice
4 tbsp. cornstarch
1½ cups boiling water
1 tbsp. ~~sugar~~ butter
10 tbsp. sugar
Small pinch salt
1 nine inch baked pie shell

———

Put yolks into bowl and add
the 1½ cups sugar, lemon rind,
juice and cornstarch. Mix well.

Add a little boiling water, combine
mixture with remaining water in
top of double boiler. Cook and
stir until
thickened. Add
butter. Cool.
Put into
pie shell.
Beat
white

stiff but
not dry.
Add slowly,
while beating
the 10 tbsp.
sugar and salt.
Cover lemon pie
custard with this
and brown for 10 min.
in very hot oven.

WHEN IN DOUBT, BAKE

Nana's Lemon Meringue Pie

5 eggs, separated
1½ cups sugar
1 tbsp. grated lemon rind
¼ cup lemon juice
4 tbsp. cornstarch
1½ cups boiling water
1 tbsp. butter
10 tbsp. sugar
Small pinch salt
1 nine inch baked pie shell

*Put yolks into bowl and add the 1½ cups sugar, lemon rind,
juice and cornstarch. Mix well. Add a little boiling water,*

combine mixture with remaining water in top of double
boiler. Cook and stir until thickened. Add butter. Cool. Put
into pie shell. Beat whites stiff but not dry. Add slowly,
while beating, the 10 tbsp. sugar and salt. Cover lemon
custard with this and brown for 10 mins. in very hot oven.

. . .

When in doubt, bake.

I didn't come up with this concept; people have
been doing oven therapy for ages. Mom says that Nana
baked constantly during that first winter in Saratoga.
It kept the house warm and her from going crazy.

When I'm so anxious that my atoms are vibrating
visibly, I bake bread. I read in a cookbook that to get
a flakier loaf, you punch the dough down more each
time it rises. For me, the process is reversed: the
flakier I get, the more I punch the dough down. But
that's for extreme cases of anxiety. For more average or
ongoing stress, I prefer making sweet things, like cake,
muffins, or pie.

. . .

My fertility acupuncturist and I talked about a lot of things—movies, the weather, Zen Buddhism. He was a funny guy, and our conversations would have been fine cocktail chatter if I hadn't been lying on a table with my bra and panties strategically covered by towels while he stuck pins into my body.

"I'll tell ya, that last scene in *GoodFellas* . . . ," he said as he flicked a pin into my foot. "And then when he says . . ." Pins in the belly now, all around the womb, flick flick flick. "BAM! And he's dead in the trunk . . ." And BAM, a pin to my head, right where the third eye is supposed to be. That's the only one I ever really felt; my acupuncturist did great "insertions," as he called his voodoo routine.

Yes, we talked about a lot of things, my fertility acupuncturist and I, just not much about the reason I kept coming back to see him. Twice a week, on Mondays and Thursdays, I'd return to his office to keep whatever eggs I had left in good shape and my period regular. On that last score, we were too successful.

I realize I'm asking too much of him the day I'm getting dressed and I pick a white hair off my black turtleneck. I wonder how one of my mother's hairs could have gotten onto my sweater and survived both the washer and dryer. Then I realize that this is one of mine.

. . .

Nana married when she was twenty-one, but she didn't become pregnant for a while; her doctors had advised her against it because of a heart condition she'd had from a young age, something she had in common with her namesake grandmother. Nana wrote that her earliest memory was of crawling up on the bed to the frail, white-haired woman, propped up on pillows, who called her "my little pussycat." Matilde survived multiple pregnancies, but Nana was told she might not live through even one:

When I was 25 I did become pregnant and didn't tell anyone until I was in the fourth month. My physician was furious with me and told me that I'd done a very foolish thing. He had me visit a cardiologist, who advised a therapeutic abortion, as it would be very risky for me to

178

have a child. I was adamant—I wanted a child and went
ahead with the pregnancy. Other than some morning
sickness, I never became ill, and my beautiful daughter
was born without incident.

That was my mother. Nana didn't tempt fate again.

Mom had me when she was twenty-one, and there are no photos from her quickie wedding. She was always honest with me about the fact that I was a surprise, because she saw no point in lying to a kid who could tell there was no love lost between her divorced parents. On my thirty-fifth birthday, Mom laughed as she told the story of going to the hospital and getting wedged in the cab between the backseat and the front when the nervous cabbie made a short stop. Looking back from an adult perspective, I knew she'd never had it easy as a young single mother, and I also knew she'd had a choice in the matter.

"Why did you have me?" I asked suddenly.

Mom thought for a moment, still smiling from the cab story. "I don't know," she finally said, but the look on her face showed that she was pleased with the outcome.

Both Nana and I were raised by our grandfathers. Hers died when she was fourteen, and mine when I was thirteen. My mother didn't remarry until I was seventeen, when she finally found the right man, a man who was not my father by blood but who became something far more important to me: my dad. One of the most loving things he could ever have said to me, a pained and irascible teenager, was "Where the hell do you think you're going at ten o'clock at night?" This was something Grandpa would have said. Here was a man who cared about me, and who told me so in the lovingly blunt language of my people.

All turned out well, but the absence of a father figure between Grandpa and my new dad left its mark on me. When I started thinking about marriage and children, I vowed I'd wait for a man who would stick around and be a husband and a father. I didn't realize that, in my case, waiting for the former might mean having to give up on the latter.

. . .

When I was thirty-seven, my gynecologist told me, "If you want to have a baby, it's now or never."

This was not the kind of thing I wanted to hear when my legs were in stirrups and there was a plastic speculum lodged in what I'd hoped would one day be part of a baby-construction site. "Uh . . . my boyfriend doesn't want to have kids," I admitted.

"Well, if *you* do, you should find a new boyfriend fast."

"Let me get this straight," I said, shifting my bare butt on the crinkly paper covering the exam table when she removed the speculum. "You're telling me to break up with my boyfriend, find a new one ASAP, and get pregnant, all within the space of a year—that's your professional advice?"

She shrugged and pulled off her rubber gloves with a snap of finality. "All I'm saying is, you're running out of time."

I ended up getting a new gynecologist before I got a new boyfriend, and by the time I met Nathan, when I was forty-one and he was forty-three, we'd both given up on the idea of having children.

But this new committed love made us hopeful. One day, I asked him, "What if we tried to have a baby?"

He thought about it for a moment and said, "Then I guess we should discuss names."

"Okay, what should we call the baby—if we have one?"

"Tex."

"What if it's a girl?"

"I meant Tex if it's a girl," Nathan said.

From then on, we referred to our future baby as Tex. Even though I was a statistical long shot, we were officially Trying. And why not? As my mother said, "If you could find a smart, sexy, straight, available man—in New York, and you over *forty*, no less—anything is possible."

.   .   .

Two years of trying the good old-fashioned way resulted in a few near misses in the form of periods that came late and heavy. I decided to seek help from an acupuncturist. Twice a day I drank a mixture of Chinese herbs designed to keep my childbearing hormones active. It tasted like someone had swept up the forest floor and made a brew of it, but I distracted myself as I gulped it down by thinking of middle names that would go with Tex. Twice a week I played human pincushion at the acupuncturist's office. At least twice a month someone would encourage me with a story about a woman over forty years old they knew, or had heard of, who'd gotten pregnant without IVF. (Nathan and I had discussed the in vitro option, but our hearts weren't in it.) I added a specialist to the team. Two times we did what we called the "March of the Penguins": Nathan "delivered" his contribution to our effort into a sterile plastic cup, which I would then shove into my bra to keep warm as I raced to be artificially inseminated at my fertility doctor's office on the Upper East Side of Manhattan—not far from where Mom brought me up by herself, and the same neighborhood where Matilde had lain bedridden after thirteen pregnancies.

And every month, I got my period.

. . .

Suzan's Execution (in every sense of the word)
of Nana's Lemon Meringue Pie

5 eggs, separated
1 ½ cups sugar
1 tbsp. grated lemon rind
¼ cup lemon juice (not tart enough: do about ⅓ cup)
4 tbsp. cornstarch

1½ cups boiling water (?? Seems like a lot . . .)
1 tbsp. butter
10 tbsp. sugar
Small pinch salt
1 nine inch baked pie shell (Can I use a store-bought one?)

Put yolks into bowl and add the 1½ cups sugar, lemon rind, juice, extra juice, and cornstarch. Mix well. Add a little boiling water, but don't combine mixture with remaining water even though it's in Nana's instructions because it just seems like too much. Pause to vacuum up shards of glass from breaking lid of double boiler. Cook and stir, losing patience when mixture refuses to thicken. Transfer mixture from double boiler to regular metal pot—okay, NOW it's thickening! Add butter and salt because mixture still tastes too sweet. Remember that you have a head cold and taste buds are off. Argh. Cool mixture. Pour into proudly home-baked pie shell (hooray for me!). Using a fork, beat whites stiff but not dry. Wonder why whites won't stiffen, dry, or even maintain a decent level of froth, and switch to a whisk. Beat them more. Beat them senseless. Become frustrated and put whites in blender. Tell husband that you know very well his mother used an eggbeater, thank you for the information, and so would you if you had one. Dump

liquid meringue down the sink and only then recall a
friend saying something about adding a pinch of cream of
tartar to egg whites. Ask husband if he'll settle for a lemon
tart. Admire his diplomacy when he assures you that the
pie is fine the way it is.

. . .

How did she do it? How did Nana get those egg
whites to form perfect peaks, which she'd then let
toast to golden brown perfection in that ancient
hearth in Saratoga? How had she found the courage
to risk her life to have a baby? Maybe she did it
because she saw the day when she and her four-year-
old daughter would go outside to those overgrown
berry bushes on the farm in Saratoga and pick tiny
wild strawberries to put on top of the meringue when
the pie had cooled. Maybe she knew there would
come a time when her daughter's daughter would sit
in a kitchen and hear how sweet the strawberries
tasted on that pie.

. . .

"What are we doing wrong?" Nathan asked, his voice
catching.

"Nothing," I said. "Nothing at all. We're fine." It was the truth; we were fine, I realized. We were fine before we started trying, and we would be again, when we went back to just being.

I said good-bye to my doctors. I gave up drinking forest tea. And now I stop trying to beat egg whites that, for whatever reason, aren't meant to be meringues.

. . .

FEBRUARY 2009

HUDSON COUNTY, NEW JERSEY

I take the lemon pie from the oven. Without the meringue topping, it's fairly glowing from the egg yolks in the curd and the butter in the crust. I bring the tart close to my face; it's warm. I sniff: tangy, sweet. It even makes tiny crackling noises as it continues to bake, a group of formerly separate ingredients humming together to form something new. I put it on the kitchen counter and wait for it to cool.

I know now that there were many things Nana wanted to do in her life—go to college, become a teacher like Miss Bumstead, be a writer, and at the very least stop having to worry about money. And there are probably some other things I don't know about because she made a practice of acceptance. If she was able to change her situation, she did. If she wasn't, she did the best she could and didn't waste time complaining. *How're you doing, Tillie? Fabulous, never better.* This is yet another lesson I have learned from her that will serve me well, in this case especially.

I had always pictured the day when I would pass my family's stories down to my child. I imagined telling Tex about Matilde masking applesauce as she admired her new vases. And about Carrie, who quietly served a fried round steak and a boiled potato to her husband every night before he went to the bar. And about the wrenching irony of Riordan, lying in a hospital bed after a drunken fall with his estranged daughter Matilda by his side, saying to the nurse, "Look at my baby—did you ever see a daughter who looked that much like her old man?" And about Grandpa broiling the bluefish he'd just caught for us, or how Mom did my hair on my wedding day while my dad watched *Old Yeller* on TV and wept . . .

Now I have to accept that, for whatever reason, this isn't meant to be.

There will always be a sadness in me over this, but it won't cancel out the joy I feel over what I do have. The love between me and Nathan fills this house. We have people, family as well as friends who are as close as blood, with whom we build more love. And I've had the privilege of spending thousands of days following my heart's desire and making a living from it.

My family may have reached the end of the line, but they will be with me always, through hard times and good. And they sit with me now in the kitchen.

Nathan and I share a slice of the tart that had hoped to be a pie, and I wouldn't change a thing.

16

FABULOUS, NEVER BETTER

Mom's Meatloaf

3 lbs. ground beef

Saltines or similar crackers

2 eggs

1 cup milk

Salt and pepper

2 large green peppers

2 medium-sized onions

Butter or olive oil for sautéing

About a quarter-pound of button mushrooms, sliced

1 large can diced tomatoes

1 large jar prepared spaghetti sauce

Put three pounds of ground meat in a large bowl. "Your grandpa liked to use chopped chuck," Mom says. "He was a big believer in the power of fat. I use chopped sirloin, which is leaner. But when we really didn't have much money, we used chuck too." *Make a bowl shape in the middle of the ground meat and add saltine crackers.*

"How many?" I ask.

"Um . . ." Mom looks at the amount she's holding. "About a handful. A good handful."

Crumble the crackers by hand and add to mixture. Beat the eggs and add them on top of the crackers, then pour in the cup of milk. Season with a few shakes of salt and pepper and smush everything together with your hands.

Cut the peppers into one-inch chunks and chop the onions. Sauté peppers and onions in a small pan with a tablespoon of butter or olive oil until just tender, about five minutes. Add about a third of this to the meatloaf mixture and set the rest aside for the gravy.

In a separate bowl, crush a generous handful or so of saltine crackers. Form two large or three small loaves out of meatloaf mixture and roll each in crushed crackers to coat. Melt about a teaspoon of butter or olive oil in a large, deep pan and brown meatloaves over medium heat for about fifteen minutes or so, then flip

with a long spatula to brown the other side, covering
with lid both times.

While loaves are browning on the second side, sauté
sliced mushrooms in a teaspoon of butter or olive oil, about
five minutes. In a medium-sized pot, combine a large can
of diced tomatoes, a jar of prepared spaghetti sauce, the
mushrooms, and the rest of the sautéed peppers and
onions. Stir and let simmer for a few minutes, then pour
over meatloaves. Cover pan, turn heat down to low, and let
loaves cook through, about an hour. Serve with blanched
green beans and white rice.

MARCH 2009
WESTCHESTER, NEW YORK

"Nana wore *black* to her wedding?"

"That was her color back then," Mom says, crushing
the crackers with a fork. "She wore a black dress and a
little hat with a black veil, and she and Grandpa were
married in a Catholic church in the neighborhood."

"I thought Nana was Lutheran . . ."

"Her family was," Mom says. "And at some point,
one of the cousins became Presbyterian, so Nana
tried that. For a while, she was Lutheran and

Presbyterian—she liked to say she was 'Loose-beterian.' Then she met Grandpa, who was Catholic, so she went to his church. When we lived in Saratoga, we went to the local Holy Roller church led by the Reverend Curtis and his wife, Aunt Miney—that's what everyone called her, Aunt Miney. Reverend Curtis would say, 'Someone among us has been fornicating—does this sinner want to come forward?' And all us kids would get wide-eyed. We didn't know what fornicating was, but based on the look on the parents' faces, it wasn't good. Then, someone would come down the aisle, sobbing and saying, 'Yes, yes, it was *me!*' And Aunt Miney would say, 'Okay, children, go outside for playtime.' She and Curtis were much better orators than fund-raisers, and they got pretty thin in the winter. So Nana and Grandpa brought them bread and chicken and vegetables, and Reverend Curtis would say, 'Thanks to Brother Charles and Sister Matilda for the kind donation of food.' That started the rest of the congregation bringing them something every Sunday, so after that, Curtis and Miney were okay.

"Anyway, at some point, Nana decided that any house of worship—church, temple, whatever—worked when she wanted to say a prayer. Later, she said prayers wherever she was, and she didn't feel the need to identify herself as belonging to any one particular faith or another. She just believed."

As I slice the mushrooms ("Not too thin," warns Mom) I try to remember how we got on the subject of Nana's daring choice of wedding dress or her open-armed spirituality. I can't, and it doesn't matter. I've learned that there's a difference between showing up for dinner at my parents' house and making dinner with my mother: as the ingredients go into the food, the stories come out of the making.

- - -

MARCH 2009
HUDSON COUNTY, NEW JERSEY

I knew it was going to be a good day when I found half a banana waiting for me on the cutting board instead of sitting in the garbage.

Nathan watches the news every morning while he eats breakfast, but today we make an executive decision to limit our intake of negativity and hysteria, and we turn the TV off. What little we saw, though, was good: It's going to be almost 65 degrees today.

After breakfast, I race outside, leaving behind my hat, thick gloves, parka, and the rest of the abominable snowwoman getup I've been wearing for months (sometimes indoors). Snowstorms could still come— we aren't done with winter yet—but I can't think about that right now because there's warm sun on my face.

At the corner I run into Arthur, the bull terrier from downstairs, straining at his leash. He bounds up to me, jaws agape and ready to clamp onto my hand—with love, but a loving clamp is still a clamp. I hold up a finger and say, "Ouch, Arthur," the code phrase his mommies taught him. The dog quickly closes his mouth and nuzzles my hand instead. "Oh, you are such a good boy!" I tell him, and he wags his stubby little tail.

Reluctantly, I return home, but for a good reason: I actually have an assignment to work on. At lunchtime I have a root beer and a sandwich made from leftover meatloaf, which is even better the next day, while I write.

A few months ago I thought things couldn't get worse. Now, I feel fabulous—never better.

Nothing has changed. There's still a lot of fear in the air, and rightly so. The life we knew before the collapse continues to melt and change, and people we know who once made good livings take jobs as nannies, look into food stamps, leave their homes and move in with friends, and wait, and hope.

But I feel no sense of loss. If anything I've gained something over these past few months as I learned to cook and found out where, and who, I came from. I think about Nana as a scared but determined kid working during the Depression, and Grandpa living through the war, and my family heading down to Florida with nothing but a hundred bucks and a hundred hopes, and Mom saving every available dime in that coffee can, and I feel better. I think to myself, *If they got through that, we can get through this.* And it wasn't all bad—sometimes what looked at first like more rotten luck turned out to be fate's little crooked smile.

In 1952, when my mother was ten years old, there was a major slowdown in construction, so Charlie was out of work more often than not. Nana saw an ad in the paper for a typist at the Triborough Bridge and Tunnel Authority, and she decided to apply for the job.

She was a little rusty after years of being a stay-at-home mom. The reports she had to type were done with layered carbon paper to make copies, and at first Nana made mistakes. Not wanting anyone to see all the pages in the trash, she took them with her into the ladies' room and stuffed them in her girdle. Mom said that when Nana came home from her first day at work, she looked like she'd gained fifteen pounds.

But she was soon hired full-time, and Nana loved that job. She worked with Robert Moses and others who were shaping New York, and she climbed the ladder higher than she'd ever thought she could go. She went from being a temp typist who had one dress (and a girdle with sturdy elastic) to an executive assistant whose wardrobe included a floor-length black fringed gown and other glamourous items, which she wore when her bosses took her along to fancy cocktail parties and white-tie dinners. She may not ever have become a published author, but she was able to use her intelligence and creativity, and she was held in high esteem by those she worked with. And she never got rich, but she was finally secure. She worked at the Coliseum very happily, right up until the day she died.

The funeral home had to open a second adjoining room to accommodate all the visitors. And then a third for the endless arrangements of flowers. People

attending other funerals poked their heads in and
asked, "Who's in there? A dignitary?"

"Yes," said Nana's boss.

.　.　.

I don't say formal prayers, but every night, I make
a mental list of things I'm grateful for. Tonight, as
always, I'm grateful for Nathan, who's snoring away
beside me, and for the knowledge that my parents are
healthy and whole, worried about their business but
generally in good spirits. I give thanks for the spring
rains breaking and for the end of the leaks pouring into
the living room. I say thank you to Nana and Grandpa
and tell them I love them. I'm grateful that I got to go
to college—I was the first woman in my family to do
so—and that I became a writer—that I've been able to
realize almost all of Nana's dreams, the ones I never
knew she had until I found the recipe file. Now she's
inspiring me to go further, to aim higher than I thought
I could go. Who knows, maybe I'll even become a
teacher like her beloved Miss Bumstead . . .

There's more, so much more that I'm grateful for,
that I start falling asleep before I can finish.

I want for nothing. I feel rich.

17

LEAVE THE DISHES

A small piece of advice, and one of the best, that I've gotten from Nana, who died at the age of fifty-seven— too young, but having never wasted a moment of her life:

I was not, and am not, the best housekeeper in the neigh-borhood. The competition of getting the first line of wash out on Monday morning has never interested me. Putting the dishes in the sink "until later" was, and still is, my practice. There are so many more important things than dishes.

Sometimes the house is such a mess that I think, "On Saturday I must do this—or that—or whatever is most in need of doing." But when Saturday comes along, and it is a delightful, delicious day, and my husband says, "Let's the three of us go fishing," we all look at each other—guiltily—and of course they stick me with the decision.

I look at the house, at their faces, at what is outside of our hazy windows and, knowing we are all only here for an unknown time, and how precious every minute is, I say: "Let's go."

ACKNOWLEDGMENTS

I make a gratitude list every day. Here is the one from the last day of writing this book.

I'm grateful to, and for:

Amy Gross, Susan Reed, Deborah Way, Pat Towers, Cathleen Medwick, Sudie Redmond, and all my editor-teachers at "Harvard." Mary Ann Naples, the right agent at the right time, and everyone at The Creative Culture. Kris Puopolo, Todd Doughty, Bill Thomas, and everyone on the Doubleday Dream Team.

Sherri Rifkin, for all the plans we made at The Happiest Place on Earth, and for giving me the occasional kick in the butt with a slingback Manolo. Francesco Clark, for breathing with me. Jon Barrett, my Guardian Angel in Chief. Aaron Krach, Muse at

Large. Amanda Siegelson, Web Mistress. Steve Korté, Superhero. Carolina Miranda, for encouragement. Susannah Harte, for patience and spiritual generosity. Gerri Brownstein, for guidance. David Keeps, for taking on an extra intern in the summer of 1984 and teaching me how to write for magazines, and who turned out to be an even better friend (and match-maker) than mentor.

The Ladies of The Grange, for sharing your recipes.

My family—relations by blood and marriage, steps and halves, and friendship beyond compare. I love you all.

And Mom, Dad, Nathan, Nana, and Grandpa: You are my heart.

ABOUT THE AUTHOR

SUZAN COLÓN is a contributing writer and editor
for *O, The Oprah Magazine*. Her essays and articles
have appeared in *Marie Claire*, *Harper's Bazaar*,
Rolling Stone, *Details*, and other magazines.
For more information, visit her Web site at
www.cherriesinwinter.com.